BEFORE DAWN

A Time of Testing, Humbling, Suffering, and Sacrificing

BEFORE DAWN

A Time of Testing, Humbling, Suffering, and Sacrificing

RALPH RILEY COOLEY

ARPress
ILLUMINATING IDEAS, EMPOWERING VOICES

ARPress
45 Dan Road Suite 5
Canton MA 02021
Hotline: 1(888) 821-0229
Fax: 1(508) 545-7580

Ordering Information:
Quantity sales. Special discounts are available on quantity purchases by corporations, associations, and others. For details, contact the publisher at the address above.

Printed in the United States of America.

ISBN-13:	Softcover	979-8-89330-549-4
	eBook	979-8-89330-551-7
	Hardcover	979-8-89330-550-0

Library of Congress Control Number: 2024900768

Table of Contents

FOREWORD

I have always wanted to write a book or memoirs about my life, but I thought that I would never get started. I would labor on the thought that my life had not been influential enough. Because, you see, I grew up on a farm, way out in the open country. But when I retired from the US Air Force, I got a job in an acute psychiatric hospital. I worked as a psychiatric nurse aid or mental health worker. That's when I started listening to Christian radio. And between the two events of my psychiatric work experience and listening to Christian radio, I can't recall all the sad stories of people's lives that I heard. Certain Christian radio host would encourage their listeners to write their own life story, adding that your story might help someone to overcome or understand a bad situation in their life. Then, a few years ago, I heard President Bill Clinton say on television that, "everyone who is fifty-five years old or older has a book or two in them." And I believed him.

But sometimes, it shames; sometimes, it pains to lay yourself bare before the world while writing your life's story. Especially when you were as poor as the dessert dirt of the earth as I was. And, even though it hurts, I felt obligated to write anyway. You know? I thought it would be interesting to tell how my mother suffered during my birth. She didn't have to endure the pain that almost took her life. She could have done it another way. But my mother chose to bear the excruciating pain, to give me a chance to live, and there was no charge!!!

Then there was the challenge of growing up on a farm. Growing up on a farm, for me, was the essence of being poor, brokenness, hard work, and missing valuable days out of school. It felt like the brokenness you feel when you have just lost your best friend, and you have just climbed to the top of heartbreak hill. But when you come face to face with it, there was value in growing up on the farm. You learned discipline. You learned the truth in the voice of your father and mother who taught you to respect your elders, to respect authority, and to respect the rights of other. You learned something about the birthing process, when farm animals were born. You learned safety in handling a team of horses, or a team of mules. You also learned to safely operate tractors, and trucks, and farm-related equipment. On the farm, we helped each other, as we practiced, leaning on the Lord.

As valuable, and as necessary as those initiatives were, I wanted to increase my role in life. So, I looked at life early. I wondered if the clanging chains that had me bound to staying out of school and sharecropping could be broken. Because my young, non-judgmental heart was set on seeking out what my true calling in life was, if, I could break free. *If I could just break free*, maybe, someday, someway, I could help someone else. You think? So I left home at age sixteen. My mother was weeping and praying for my safety as I headed north, on Georgia highway 113, hitch hiking, thumbing a ride. I was looking for a place that I could have consistent time in school, but hitch hiking was awful that day.

I tried to hitch a ride on a big, heavily loaded green and yellow Mack truck way back by the church, up on raccoon hill. The driver sadly waved me off; he kept on shifting, and jamming, lower, and stronger gears. He was struggling trying to climb raccoon hill. After the Mack passed me, there was no traffic on the road. So I walked and I walked. I walked all the way up past the dead man's curve. And before long, a free-wheeling trucker came by. I had never seen him running highway 113 before. I hitched a ride with him anyhow. A nice man he was; he was concerned about me being out there on that dangerous highway alone. And, in just a few minutes, we were rolling into the city limits of Cartersville, Georgia. I got off at a little store near Aubrey Street, just down the hill from Summer Hill High School. After school, I found the place that had been set-aside for me to stay and go to school.

When I finished high school, I went into the service. This was a gigantic step for me. I appeared to have been pretty selfish at the beginning of basic training. I was dreadfully introverted. But the Lord told me, well, it must have been the Lord who told me, that, if I didn't start sharing my light freely with others, I would surely die right there in basic training. Then, a young airman in my flight came un-invited to shadow me, to learn my every strength, and my every weakness. He did this so that if I were ever beset by an emergency, someone would know me well enough to save my life. That emergency did come. He and others helped me get through it. I went on through basic training, and was given my career field assignment.

I was assigned to the petroleum career field. The petroleum career field is totally safety and security orientated. It's skillful. It is busy. Its one hundred percent mission essential, and the petroleum career field is very, very political. It demands good character, loyalty, perseverance, and unwavering dedication to duty. By naturally displaying these traits, I literally went from the cotton field to some very important assignments with the United States Air Force. As a young airman in the early 1960s, I was heavily involved in servicing B-52-G model bombers of the Strategic Air Command (SAC), with hundreds of thousands of pounds of JP-4 jet fuel. They were air borne for twenty-four consecutive hours.

These bombers were employed in the deterrence of the Mutually Assured Destruction (MAD), phase of the cold war with Russia. Then there was Air Force One. In the mid 1960s, I was handpicked, security cleared, and assigned as a refueling supervisor with the first airplane to be so designated as Air Force One. This aircraft was commissioned for Presidents. President John F. Kennedy first flew on the aircraft in November 1962. I was also blessed to have been assigned to the largest Tactical Fighter Wing in the U.S. Air Force, and possibly the world. I was assigned as fuels superintendent. Part of my duties there were as negotiator, coordinator, and writer on the Joint Support Planning (JSP) team for the 81st Tactical Fighter Wing, and the North Atlantic Treaty Organization (NATO). This was an arm of intelligence (Intel), and of war planning. Our work with the JSP team helped to end the cold war. These events were sometimes disarming. And yes, sometimes refreshing. God's favor was no doubt with me. But what will be the final bill, or the final pay off, for all the pain and suffering found on the foregoing pages of this documentthis book, Before Dawn?

Ralph Riley Cooley

ACKNOWLEDGEMENTS

First, I would like to thank God for choosing life for me and giving me hope when things were, not going so well for me. I thank him for the joy of living. I want to thank my mother for bearing the excruciating pain to bring me into this world. I thank her for her tears and prayers because I know that through her prayers, she snatched me from the depths of the oceans, and the angry seas. Mother was always my number one confidant. I would like to thank my dad for being such an energetic worker, and for trying so hard to pull his family up. I would also like to thank my dad for showing up at my baseball games on Sundays with his overalls and white Sunday shirt on. He always came close to home plate when I was at bat to cheer me on.

I would like to thank my brothers and sisters for helping me in my infancy when I could not help myself. I would also like to thank my siblings, and friends for their love, care, and companionship during my maturation years. Many thanks to Daddy B., Mama Zadie, and Grand Ma Ella for so lovingly and willingly taking me in at age sixteen so I could go to school. I would like to thank Professor and Mrs. Morgan and family for giving me a job, mostly working their gardens, cutting grass, washing their cars, doing house work, and driving for them so I could have a little spending money during the school season.

I would like to thank the US Air Force for giving me the chance to reach for the stars. I would like to thank all of my Air Force superiors, contemporaries, and subordinates for their love of country, dedication, and their help through the United States Air Force to make the world a better place.

I would like to thank my wife, for so willingly, and skillfully adapting to the military way of life. She was an excellent homemaker and nurturer for the family. She quietly embraced the somewhat frequent moves, and the children changing schools. She cheerfully maintained gainful employment at every station to enhance family economics. She helped make the eight years that we served in Europe an unforgettable, pleasant, and educational journey. I would also like to thank my wife for giving me a break from continually working in her several flower gardens while trying to finish this book. I would like to thank my son, Reggie, for his expert work keeping the computers operating. I would like to thank my son, Carl, for his prayers, and kind words from a distance all the way from the state of Oregon. I would like to thank my grandson, Jamal, for his technical work, and computer savvy. I would also like to thank Jamal for his encouraging review of the work.

I would like to thank my brother, Perry, for validating the truth about an important character in the book, Miss Dolly. I would like to thank my brother, Carey, for walking a mile with me with my badly sprained ankle when we were little. I thank Carey for his interest in the book. And, also, I would like to thank my sisters, Earlene, Betty, and Levon (Bonnie) for their consistent excellence in character and for their enthusiastic reviews, and helpful comments about this work.

I would like to thank my niece, Monica Gober, for her whole-hearted belief in the book's worthiness to be published and well marketed. My family is very important to me. Even though I have been away, except for a few short visits, here and there about fifty-six years now. But they didn't forget me, even the children. God blessed nine of my eleven siblings to have children; beautiful children. They taught those children, to the fourth generation, to know their uncle Ralph. And when I come home, they come by to see me, as many as they can. For this, I thank you forever. Sometimes, I feel like I'm the lost one because I've been out there on the wind for so long. But while out there on the wind, I passed by so many places that I had never passed that way before. I thank God and family for that. I would like to thank Steve, Lora, Mike, and Marino from the Portsmouth Library for their kind, willing, and professional device help. Likewise, I would like to thank the staff at Staples office supplies and computers. Special thanks to Seth Burton, Michael, Skip, and Dan for their skillful assistance on the latest developments and operations of computers. 'I feel very special that Christian Faith Publishing elected to publish my book. The staff is very kind and very superior. My assigned publication specialist, Cassandra Byham, thru her outstanding communicative skills kept me interacting with the special publishing teams, who valued my input throughout the entire publishing process. Thanks Christian Faith Publishing you are simply the best.

Ralph Riley Cooley

1

Trouble in the Womb

Sometimes, the very sound of a telephone ringing can indicate something is terribly wrong. Still I answered.

"Mom is dead," my sister said through tears.

I couldn't speak. Yet, before we hung up, I'd volunteered to speak at the funeral, The news of my mother's death had pierced my heart so deeply I didn't know if I could make it through the night, much less make through the service. But at the appointed time, I stood up, walked to the front of the church, squeezed the podium, and spoke words of comfort my precious mother taught me as a child.

"(The Lord is my shepherd I shall not want. He maketh me to lie down in green pastures. He Leadeth me beside the still waters. He restoreth my soul. He leadeth me in the path of righteousness for his name's sake. Yeah though I walk through the valley of the shadow of death I will fear no evil. For thou art with me…"

I paused and looked down at the woman who enabled me to stand; the woman who loved me when no one else did. She took ugly and made a beautiful life, my life. In a flash, I remembered everything. In a flash, I remembered what my family told me what happened when I was born. According to them, I caused horrifying pain while in my mother's womb long before dawn. Before I could break free and come forth into this world, it was before dawn. And before my gentle mother could dress me in my first lovely garments or feed me, it was before dawn. Not because it was before the light of day begun, for the sun had rose somewhere in the east to give it's light to the day. It was before dawn because I didn't have time to take one unrestrained breath to begin my lot in life, neither did I have time to stand on my own two feet before the days of trouble came.

Trouble came early; trouble came indeed, before dawn. My older brother, Glenn, indicated that during my birth, I was afraid. He told me that I was so afraid that I tried not to come out and meet the world. "You caused her so much pain," he said, "you almost killed my mother." Glenn's remarks seemed so cutting and so dark. But Glenn never meant for his remarks to be cutting and dark. He must have been feeling our mother's pain. You recon? Because he knew that I took no pleasure in being a troubled birth for that was before dawn. And in reality, it's always darkest before dawn, isn't it?

During the birthing process, something went wrong in my mother's birth canal. This made my birth very difficult. Hello. My name is Ralph Riley Cooley. "Riley," my middle name, came about to honor Dr. Riley. Dr. Riley saved my mother's life and allowed my birth to become a reality. Due to Dr. Riley's skillful hands and integrity in his work, my daddy insisted that some part of my name would be to honor the doctor. Dr. Riley worked for hours trying to figure out what went wrong.

Dr. Riley and others worked so long, in fact, that many people gave up on me ever seeing the sun. They were thinking that I would miss all of the excitement and adventures of living. Yet, others were saying that it would have been better for me, if I had been still born, rather than to have lived. My delayed birth with all of its difficulties, however, gave me a little more time in the womb alone with my dear protective mother, and my heavenly creator. I needed the time.

It didn't matter the measure of time it took for the doors of her womb to release their grip-on me; my mother was determined. She was determined to give without taking. Even though the struggle and labor pains almost took my mother's life, my loving mother gave me birth without taking my life. My birth was truly a labor of love. My birth came on March 15, 1941 in the same month and on the same date as my mother's birth, thirty-six years earlier. My mother's labor of love did not come without issues. Some of the issues were, my body was badly bruised with black and blue abrasions all over it. My skin was very dark and it was rusty in places. My face was abnormally ill formed.

Because of these issues, my outward appearance was ugly. And because of my ugly outward appearance, I was outwardly scorned and secretly abused. Through it all, there was much misery, and much need for assistance. My Mother was bed ridden for a period of time after my birth. Therefore, she was limited in her daily activities. Mother was unable to be close by when visitors, some of whom were strangers, wanted to hold me. And when some of the strangers would hold me, I would cry. I would cry so loud; and I would cry so sad, they said, that some visitors and my mother were alarmed. My mother was so alarmed that she pondered if my outward appearance might be an issue because this never happened with any of her other eight children, for they were born beautiful. However, in my case, there was no beauty to look upon.

In my mother's effort to protect me from further agony, she instructed my older siblings to draw near to me and investigate what was causing my miserable behavior. My older siblings' investigations held that some of the visitors who were strangers were making me miserable. They were pinching me. I was too ugly to love! Upon learning this, my mother had me presented by only trusted friends and my older siblings. When my mother had me presented to visitors by only trusted friends and my older siblings, the crying stopped. My mother was heavenly esteemed, and she vowed that I should never forget any of my siblings who bore my burdens and protected me. Mother would remind me as I got older who there were:

Horace Jr.–sixteen Catherine–fourteen
James–twelve
Glenn–ten
Earlene–six
Betty P.–four
Perry–two
Elma Jo–deceased at age two

Despite my sibling's unyielding help, my troubles were not over yet. Yes, the world is full of trouble, my dear mother submitted when she learned that I would have to wear a truss because of my navels maldevelopment. A truss is a supportive device worn to prevent enlargement of a hernia or the return of a reduced hernia. My truss consisted of a brown cloth belt that held a big brown medicine ball over my bulging navel. While it was necessary for me to wear that discovery, it was not kind. It was worrisome, and it slowed me down. That truss slowed me down so much, especially when I would run and play. Sometimes, I would run and play so long and so rugged that the truss would fall off of my bulging navel. When this would happen, the older children would have to secure it again. When they would tire of securing the truss again and again, they would bring me in the house to mother, and I would cry. I would cry because I longed to be with the other children, especially the children who would sometimes visit us. With tears streaming down my face, mother would comfort me saying, "you have played long enough for one day my child. Please come and let us try to get you well. We want to get you well so hopefully you can father children of your own someday."

Then mother would take me in her tender arms and rock me to sleep. I could have slept in her loving arms forever. But there was not much time for a lot of sleeping because we were a large family of hard working North Georgia sharecroppers.

Sharecroppers were mostly poor people living on the land. They usually planted, nurtured, and harvested large crops of cotton, corn, wheat, hay, and a variety of garden vegetables on the land. Sharecroppers worked the land for a landlord. The landlord furnished the fertilizer and seeds for the various crops and a pair of mules and whatever equipment was needed to tend the crops. When the crops were harvested, the landlord would take one half of the crops' yield. A landlord also would provide shelter; usually a substandard poorly maintained house or an old shack for the sharecropper's family. Landlords preferred large sharecropper families because of the vast amount of land they could work.

2

Growing Up in a Loving Country Home

It was important for sharecropper families to hold together because the larger the family, the better opportunity for their economic growth. It was also important to have both parents, and I enjoyed the precious gift of having my mother and daddy living under the same roof as long as I was at home.

My daddy was a great dad, who cared very deeply about his family. His efforts to do the best for us were hampered only by the lack of a good education. He was diligent and overly conscientious about his work. Unfortunately, though, my dad was unable to get much of an education. Dad depended on my mother to execute the business and social affairs in our home, and she did it with honor. My mother surpassed my dad in education. She used her education well. My mother handed down the rules in our home after consulting with dad. She did all of the family bookkeeping and she helped us children with our homework when there was time for school.

She filled in at times as a substitute teacher over at the two or three-room schoolhouse, and she was faithful. My mother was also a very faithful Christian woman who put God first in all of her activities. Both of my parents were very gentle, loving, and kind. This attitude carried over to my siblings. The gentle, loving, and kind spirit displayed by my family was very necessary to the sharecropper. There was so much sacrifice and so many hard ships to endure like living in substandard housing, provision for daily living was in question at times, little to no help in emergency situations, scarce transportation caused walking long distances to be a way of life, and school attendance was a low priority when certain farm work was in season.

The major priority was to labor and toil from sun up to sun down in the dark rich soil. Growing cotton and other crops could be unpleasant and dangerous work at times. We girded ourselves up with safety precautions and we depended heavily on God. I do believe God gave me the gift to do certain meaningful labor at an early age no matter how dangerous. But nevertheless, I would often get injured trying to do work that I had not quite grown in to. When I was just four years old, I would follow my family to the cotton field, and I would pick a few pounds of cotton trying to be helpful to my family.

One evening when the sun had gone down and darkness was all around us, we were coming up out of the cotton field with a wagonload of cotton. That's when I suffered my first injury. I was sitting on a sheet of cotton on top of the wagon. Due to the darkness, the mule-drawn wagon hit a big bump in the road; when the wagon hit the big bump in the road, the sheet of cotton that I was sitting on shifted. This caused me to fall off of the wagon, resulting in my left leg being run over by one of the rigid wheels on the wagon. My siblings who witnessed the accident were frantic. I was taken to the hospital that night. I did not receive an x-ray. I guess it was due to a lack of technology. Therefore, the doctor cautiously assessed my injury by moving his thumb and index finger along the bone in my leg. He did this several times. When I did not flinch and there was no sign of a fracture, the doctor determined that I was ok. We showed our appreciation to the doctor. We left the hospital and began our eleven-mile journey back home in the A-Model ford that my family borrowed from our landlord. Everyone showed much kindness and much compassion for me. Likewise, I was filled with compassion for my loving close-knit family. The kindness and compassion extended to me made me want to do even more work. So I would work and stand in the gap whenever and wherever I was able.

When I was five years old, I would take food and water to my dad. My dad would be following the plow, a half-mile or more east of our house in the dark fertile soil down in the bottomland. There were obstacles for a little boy traveling alone. One of the obstacles was the tall grass on either side of the trail leading to the fields. The grass was about waist high on me, and in some places, it was a little taller. Sometimes, strange noises wound be coming from the grass and the strange noises would baffle me. Another obstacle to carrying food and water to my dad when he was following the plow down in the bottomland was the suspicious patterns being made in the tall grass beside me. Sometimes, in the tall grass beside me, something would make slithering patterns. When the tall grass beside me would move in a slithering pattern, I would ponder why.

It was a lonely feeling. It was such a lonely feeling. For companionship and protection, I would usually carry a pocket full of stones. One day when the grass was moving in a suspicious slithering pattern, I searched for stones and found that I had no pockets. I had no pockets. I had no stones. This was troublesome, a misery on a perilous journey. I thought of turning around, but the culprit might have turned around too. My daddy would not have gotten any food that day. So I continued on my perilous journey.

I was only five years old, and I was only frightened. But the fright went away eventually. When the fright went away, these words began to flow, "The Lord is my shepherd; I shall not be in want. He makes me lie down in green pastures. He leads me beside quiet waters. He restores my soul. He guides me in the path of righteousness. Even though I walk through the valley of the shadow of death I will fear no evil for you are with me. Your rod and your staff they comfort me."

3
Share Cropping as a Way of Life

I truly felt comfort that God would lead me through the valley of the shadow of death. Like-wise, I believe my daddy felt comfort that he received food to eat and water to drink. And he was free to sit down and rest a little while. Sometimes while daddy was resting, the mules would take the plow, and me for a round or two. While he rested, I believe daddy felt comfort knowing that he and my mother were doing well, not only in farming, but in negotiating. My parents were negotiating the purchase of a parcel of the dark fertile soil that we typically tended as sharecroppers.

It was a comfortable negotiation because all of the older children were at home and my family was thriving. The landlord talked favorably about selling my family a parcel of the land that always produced big crops, but he would talk and stall. Talk and stall. He talked and stalled until the four oldest children grew tired of waiting and moved on. Then the talks changed, and then the talks stopped. The talks were gone forever. Nevertheless, daddy tried to prove himself worthy of land ownership. But his family now, much younger, was an obstacle to success.

We were twelve, ten, eight, six, four, and two years old. With this group, daddy simply could not contend with the great demands put on him. Even though each one of us six years old or older never knew idle hands, we were doing leaps over the amount of work normally expected of children our age.

Despite being over tasked, we worked as smart as we could. Sometimes, we would guess on having a bale of cotton picked and loaded on the wagon by nightfall. Therefore, we would have the mules and wagon standing by. But under the dismay of darkness, we did not always have the bale picked. So we would leave the wagon and the harnesses in the field and take the mules to the barn. Desperation. It was sheer desperation. We were desperate because we needed to get the cotton picked before the cotton bowls rotted and their contents fell to the ground. We were desperate because the children needed to get in school before the schoolhouse doors closed for the thanksgiving and Christmas holidays. We were even more desperate because we needed to secure a roof over our heads for another season. We were so needy, in fact, that our,ailing mother, when she could find the strength, would come to the field the next morning and pick.

When we about had the bale of cotton sacked, I would beg to be sent to get the mules so the older children and mother and daddy could continue picking. Sometimes I would be granted what I asked for; and when I was, I would go on my way to the barn. I was six years old. I would stop at the house just for a moment to grab some coconut stick candy.

The mules drooled over the taste of my coconut and sugar coated hands, and this gave me big pull with them even at the baby age of six. I believe the mules shared my family's sense of urgency and our advanced need for unity. Therefore, the mules were kind and cooperative with me for the most part. However, the younger mule (Alice), would declare a couple of moments of show time before accepting her bit and bridle from such a young, ever laboring soul such as I. After snorting and pawing and raring up for a while, Alice would then come to her stall door, lower her head, and take her bit and bridle. After I would get the mules bridled, I would need a safety deed. An excellent safety deed, (a tip from mother) was to attach the older mule, Mary, by her reign to Alice's bit and bridle. Now Mary would become an ally, in an emergency. Then I would climb to the top strand of the barbed wire fence and crawl on to Alice's back. And then I would ride bare back over the rises and falls of the terrain back to the field under the canopy of my mother's faithful prayers.

Mother's prayers were encouraging to us and helped us with the backbreaking work and extended responsibilities. We as a family met the backbreaking work and extended tasks such as helping weigh the cotton and loading it on the wagon head on. But we didn't know what our fate would be at the end of cotton harvest that year. Even if we had known seasons ahead, there was not anything we could have done differently to change the outcome because the landlord held our fate in his hands. And because our fate rested with him, the landlord labeled our family as a failure. And as such, he informed our daddy to start hunting for another place to move his family to. (The probability of landowner ship may have irritated the situation.) Being labeled as a failure hurt my daddy to the core.

Hurting and hunting in all the familiar places, daddy had no success in finding a new place to live in the immediate area. Therefore, we had to pull up stakes and get out. We moved several miles away from Stilesboro, GA and the dark fertile land that my family had come to know and depend on. Having to abruptly move made it very tough and teary for us, but it was a very urgent move.

As we said good-bye to our friends and neighbors, we were thinking that some day, somehow, maybe by time and miracles, we would meet again. But really, there was not much hope of ever seeing our fiends again. Because transportation was scarce and people didn't usually go very far from home in those days any way. Even though transportation was scarce, there was transportation available for us to move. On the day we were going to move, a black 1941 Dodge half ton with high side gates on it drove up and parked at our home.

After we got all of our stuff loaded on the truck, us kids climbed into the back of the truck for our parting trip. We took care to see that no one got left behind. Our dog, however, almost got left behind because he was sick. He looked so sad, and starved standing there alone. His bones were already showing. He had the mange. We called him "Rattler." Rattler looked so very sad, that our older brother, James, the driver of the truck put our dog on the back of the truck with us kids- mange and all. We were glad we didn't leave our pooch behind. We couldn't bear to think Rattler would have to sleep his last sleep without the family.

4

Moving to the Wilderness

After along and treacherous trip, we arrived at what would be our new third base, the last turn before reaching home. It was a narrow, dusty dirt road leading to a small creek with no bridge. Yes, a creek with no bridge to cross. There was a one family house on the hill just above the creek. We traveled about a quarter of a mile beside a pasture fence on the right, and there it was, an old house sitting alone at the end of the road. The house was obviously abandoned. Abandoned for years it appeared. We were home at last, but I was confused.

"Is this where we have to live?" I asked.

"This place looks like the beginning of the wilderness. How did daddy find such a, scary place?" we all asked.

Now all of this was at the end of a long, tedious journey. I wasn't sure what was worse, the journey or the house. Ours was a barren trip without anything a family needs to travel. You know, little things like food, fluids, and a bathroom. Eventually, we came to a little store at a fork in the road north west of Cartersville, Georgia. Here we got our food and fluids, but no bathroom. Our dog had better luck. He found a tree.

To grasp the terrible trip that led to an equally terrible house, you have to understand one thing. Hubert and Carey were just small boys. They were riding up front with James, mother, and daddy. Bonnie wasn't born yet. Mix young children with hunger, add a dog, a half way running truck with no bathroom, and you can probably imagine the many possibilities. Even still by the grace of God, we finally got to that area of the road I call "third base." The truck started slowing down, as we were about to turn. Mother gathered the family and gave thanks for our safe arrival. Then she asked God to lead us, and give us wisdom to adjust, and have faith that we were being obedient to him for being out in this wilderness existence. All this, it is generally held, happened because of a break down in relationships; a break down between a good man and his family trying to make progress, and their landlord. Being cast into the wilderness was extremely difficult for us. However, it did not deter our faith. Deuteronomy 8 tells us that the wilderness is a place to humble and test us to see what is in our hearts, to teach you that man does not live on bread alone, but on every word that comes from the mouth of God.

While learning about our new environment, we learned about Mr. Duffy's little store by the side of the road about two miles further on up in the wilderness. We met one of the two families that lived in the vicinity. We learned about the fields, the forests, and the pastures. We learned about the natural spring down in the pasture that continuously bubbled up cold crystal clear water. We learned the attitudes of the creeks that surrounded us. We learned that our house, which sat on a slightly elevated lot, would become an island at times. The old house would be our only refuge when the pouring rains came. An irony I will never forget. Our terror would eventually become our refuge.

The house protected us from the raging waters generated by the creeks, locking us in. When it would rain a lot, no one could go out; and no one could come in to the area. Merely watching the attitudes of nature and our observances alerted us that getting to school and back might be a problem at times. Finding the safest and shortest route to and from school was another concern while we were learning our way around in the wilderness. We were required to walk to and from school since not all school children were fortunate enough to have school busses back then. As we studied different routes, we found that they all presented with some dangers and some difficulties. The route that we chose consisted of the following as some of the dangers and difficulties.

- A pasture fence
- A cow pasture
- A creek with no bridge
- Another pasture fence
- A twenty- acre red field
- A logging road

- A cross road
- Another creek with no bridge, the creek had only a foot log
- Another logging road
- A road characterized by gray dirt, dead grass and a moderate incline.
- Wild animals and snakes

In total, we walked through the wilderness four to five miles, more or less, round trip to and from school each day in all kinds of weather conditions. People always claim to have walked such distances. We actually did.

A typical trip to school; first, we would cross a barbed wire fence that ran parallel to our front yard. Then we went down through the pasture to a small creek that had no bridge where poisonous water moccasin could be seen at times near our, crossing. We would jump across the creek if it had not been stirred to rise. Then we went on through the pasture where cattle would sometimes be grazing and or relaxing. We proceeded on across the pasture and crossed another pasture fence into a large red field used for farming.

We proceeded on from the red field south down a logging road, which led to a crossroad. At the crossroad, we met three little girls maybe twelve, nine, and six years old. These little girls were from the Mays family. They were Georgia Mae, Ella Marie, and Bobbie Sue. This meeting had been pre planned by the grown-ups of our respective families. These little girls showed us the way as we walked with them in an easterly direction down a farming/logging road through the woods. The Mays family also had two boys who would ride their bikes along the logging tracks to school after doing farm chores. The Mays boys were Wes and Boots. The logging tracks leading to our schoolhouse were rough and deep, and sometimes filled with water. We sensibly suffered our way around, across, and sometimes through them. Our muddied tracks were testaments that we had passed that way. And we didn't look back. We kept our gaze on things ahead and our minds on God above. I believe God smiled as he saw us so faithfully carrying out his determination as he watched over us. It was his determination, not ours!

At a certain point, the woods continued on the left side of the road, and a field of dried up cotton stalks lay on the right side of the road. At the edge of the field was a small house with maybe two rooms. Directly across from the small house was an abandoned saw mill. There were some strips of wood and a huge decaying saw dust pile left behind. The sawdust pile had several holes in it where foxes and perhaps other wild animals made their dens.

Some days when we passed by, there would be a red or a yellow or a silver fox sitting on top of the sawdust pile, making the area appear frightful. I often wondered if the wild animals had outbid civilized people for the area because that little house sat empty that whole school year. I also pondered who would need to live in such a small house any way. Whoever might live there, wouldn't they be lonely? Wouldn't they be afraid living in such an isolated place with woods and wild animals all around? God protect them always, because no one could hear their pleas for help in an emergency. Ok, back to the school trip. So we continued on down that old rugged road, we passed by all kinds of growth. There were, wild honey suckle vines, black berry vines, plum trees, wild cherry trees, Bermuda grass, and Johnson grass. They all stood cold, bare, and withered waiting to come alive in the spring. As the vines and the trees and the grass slept waiting to come alive in the spring time, the Mays kids that we met way back at the cross roads kept my two sisters, my brother, and me entertained and well informed. Those kids cautioned us on the ways of the wilderness and its dangers.

I think we all secretly entertained the thought of what horrific creature might be stalking, or what creatures might have need to share the roads of the wilderness with us. Maybe a bobcat, a wild pig, a wayfaring man, a mad dog, or maybe even a rattler. Rattler, such an awful thought. In fact, three large snakes were our biggest kill in one afternoon while coming home from school. On that afternoon, we killed a six-foot long black racer, and two five-foot long brown, red, and yellow rattlers. Then there was that troubled water.

The nice Mays kids proceeded to tell us about a large lake of troubled water that lay ahead. The lake had a large dam where water could flow over or under it. The run off from the dam had formed a large creek. The creek started out shallow and wide. It was too wide for little children to cross; however, though, about one hundred yards downstream from the dam, the creek banks narrowed. The creek banks narrowed to twenty to thirty feet apart, and this made it run swifter and deeper. Now that we heard of the lake, the dam, and the creek, they told us about the foot log.

"Is there a bridge across the creek?" My sisters asked

"No."

The creek has a foot log. My sisters were concerned about our safety, especially for my brother and me. My brother was nine, and I was seven.

"You all will be just fine with a little coaching. Just go slow and hold on to the hand cable." The oldest Mays daughter told us. "You all will learn; we all had to learn. Look at Bobbie Sue, she's just six, and she's still learning."

At the foot log, the Mays' oldest daughter, Georgia Mae, lined us up a big kid and a little one, a big kid and a little one, etc. We clustered in age from six to thirteen. We made our first foot log crossing safely. Then we turned right and went back into the woods and traveled along more logging roads. Subsequently, however, we did finally make it to the two-room schoolhouse. We were worn, but safe and on time. Walking to school and overcoming such obstacles became familiar, and you might say, acceptable to us. You might say it was pitiful. It made me sad to see the way we lived. It was tough and trying, but it was an honest way of living. We got through it; for we were conquerors. We were conquerors without guns or swords, but with faith and heart. Because that's the way we lived. That's just the way we lived.

5

Walking to School in the Wilderness (Miss Dolly)

Even though it made me sad to see the way we lived, though sadly we lived; we accepted our many challenges. I'd be hard pressed to believe that any children anywhere have ever been so challenged to get to and from school. But then, it made me proud that we never plotted any upward change by another's ruin or by unjust gain. It was by faith. And I believe our creator was pleased with our faithfulness. To be faithful and poor is a challenge. At times, it can be a challenge to believe in an all-knowing God who knows your desperate circumstances, yet doesn't change them. We still believe.

While little changed over time, we continued our calling to find that little schoolhouse, and a teacher, and an open school book, because of hope. We held out hope that things would get better for us over time, because after all, the sun eventually must shine. It can't rain all the time. Even with this hope, the very next school year, very little changed. The pastur, and the creek with the moccasins were still there. The big red field, the woods, and the logging tracks were still there. The crossroads were still there. The little house, the abandoned saw mill, and wild foxes were yet visible. The wild honey suckle vines and their surroundings were still there. The lake, the dam, the creek, and the much feared foot log were forever in their places. However though, later that school year, someone came to live in that little house. Everything changed forever.

Miss Dolly

We could not discern who moved into the little house because they would not show their face or their faces. However, as passers by, we learned that someone had indeed come to live deep in the wilderness; the smoke billowing up from the chimney was a tell-tale sign. We continued to see smoke billowing up from the chimney day after day, but not a shadow of human life could be seen. No one could be seen.

One afternoon, we were returning home from school. The Williams kids were walking with us that day, as they would do sometimes. In all, there were four William's kids, two teen-age girls, a little girl, and a little boy about my age. We were passing by the little abandoned house when a big woman emerged and she was coming toward us in a hurry! "Oh God!" I shouted.

The big woman had an eerie look. She had uncommonly shiny dark skin like a plum filled to tightly about to burst. She had pearly white teeth. Her eyes were as large as hen eggs. They were white some of the time, but sometimes, her eyes were as red as fire in a coal-burning stove. She wore a black head rag, a black dress, and a white apron. All this was too much. Who was this woman? Her name was Miss Dolly.

Miss Dolly seemed to have adored our company, especially the girls. She would put her hands on her hips, and she would laugh, and smile, and talk to them. Miss Dolly seemed like someone to be afraid of. I make no bones about it; I was scared to death of her. Could she have been a nice person, we reasoned, as we got to know her better? Well, she liked to play, and sometimes she would quickstep toward us little boys like she was going to take one of us away. And when she would quickstep toward us, I would run and cling to my sister's legs so tight that nothing could pry me loose.

Then Miss Dolly would laugh and say, "I's gonna catches dat dare prettys one, and keeps him out sheer in dees sheer woods wid me. Maybe hees can helps Miss Dolly."

This woman was a horror, but kind of a nice horror. She acted as if she was distressed in some manner. Maybe Miss Dolly was crying out for help because of her loneliness and fear.

Miss Dolly was so lonely and afraid that she would, in fact, tell us things when she was in a telling mood. One day when she was in a telling mood, Miss Dolly told us that she carried a weapon. Her weapon was not a conventional weapon such as a hunter or someone in authority would carry. Miss Dolly's weapon was easily concealed and it was cheap. Her weapon was simply a can of Red Devil lye, which she called her ten cents pisol (pistol). And Miss Dolly expressed confidence in using her ten cents "pisol," as she pronounced it. She had been driven to depend on such a weapon because fear and loneliness had ruled her life.

No one could understand why Miss Dolly would come to live under the dark clouds way out there in the wilderness. Who would do that on purpose? What would it prosper her? Perhaps, she came to the wilderness hunting for some one. Could the hunted one have been Jesus? Even a small boy could discern that Miss Dolly needed a comforter. Maybe the comforter, Jesus, would meet her here. But then, maybe, it was Jesus who sent her out here in the wilderness to meet a small boy, and witness his mother's teachings; that Jesus Christ is the Son of God. The small boy, "I" must be humble, compassionate, filled with wisdom and understanding. I really didn't know. I just knew Miss Dolly confused me and intrigued me at the same time.

I regret that I did not help Miss Dolly find Jesus, but I was only seven or eight. What could I have told her about Jesus anyway? I guess I could have told her about his faithfulness and how He protected my family in the worst of times. I guess I could have told her Jesus will never leave you or forsake you. I guess I should have told her, but I was afraid of her. I would learn later that I had no reason to be afraid of Miss Dolly, only because she didn't look just real or she didn't talk just right. Because every acquaintance is God ordered and God approved. And furthermore, Hebrews 13-2 says, "Do not forget to entertain strangers, for by so doing some people have entertained angels without knowing it." It seems like Miss Dolly was saying to me, "little boy, go quickly. Run and find Jesus. And when you find him, tell him that there is a woman out here in the wilderness. Tell him that she has been neglected. Tell him that she has been mistreated and troubled. Little boy, tell Jesus that there is trouble all around Miss Dolly."

"Can't you see trouble in my eyes? When my eyes are white, and natural, my worries and troubles have been few. When my eyes turn gray, I feel afraid and alone, and my right hip has been in pain for a while. I panic from shortness of breath and my eyes are over run by my bitter tears. Oh, if I could speak well, I would speak with him who heals, I would speak with him who is merciful. Little boy, before my eyes turn red, will you be my friend and speak for me? Run, little boy, and tell Jesus that my husband roams a lot. And now he is back home. Tell Jesus that when that man is at home, he treats me with scorn; tell him that, that man puts me out in the cold at midnight. When my eyes turn red, I have not slept. I am weary, and I am broken to the bone. Little boy, tell Jesus when my eyes turn red I've been, crying, I've been crying all night long." Maybe that's what she was trying to tell this little boy.

In time, her crying and sleepless nights would come to an end. And some time later, she slept. She slept her last sleep. And it is said that they found Miss Dolly's bones. They found her bones in the field or in the decaying saw dust pile near the small house that she lived in out in the woods of the wilderness. But why did Miss Dolly die?

Perhaps, her burdens were too hard to bear. It might have been that Miss Dolly's husband, Mr. Pledge, killed her and buried her bones. While the wilderness is a place of sadness, it is also a place of witness and teaching. It had already whispered and hinted to me what my calling would be through Miss Dolly. I had the chance. Even as a little boy, I should have told her. I shall tell all others. And more than that, the wilderness is a place where burden bearing and miracles are made plain.

6

The Day My Brother Slipped Off the Foot Log

When you are eight years old, you don't just wake up expecting to have to bear some one else's burdens. Neither are you thinking of seeing the most powerful miracle of your life. It's just not on an eight-year-old's schedule. On the morning of February 12, 1950, neither my daddy nor my mother were anywhere to be found. They were home the night before, but in the morning, they were gone.

Mom would wake up singing those good ole gospel songs in the morning. With her sweet tenor voice, she would sing songs such as, *Go Tell It on the Mountain That Jesus Christ Is Born, I Know It was the Blood that Saved Me, The Old Rugged Cross, Down By the Cross I Bow, and Oh How I Love Jesus Just Because He First Loved Me.* But the morning of February 12, 1950, there was not a sound. No good ole gospel to help us to get the day started. Instead, it was the voice of my sisters Earlene and Betty.

"We won't be going to school today," they said. "It will be just you and your brother Perry."

My sisters encouraged us to please hurry and get ready so we could meet the Mays kids over at the crossroads and avoid walking to school alone. I believe we could have avoided any attempt to go to school that morning with a little persuasion. A certain spirit was calling me to go on. We finally got ready, but we were still wondering where our dear mother was. Nevertheless, Perry and I started on our journey alone. We got through the barbed wire fence with just a minor nick in my nice gray mackinaw jacket. We continued on down through the pasture to the creek. The creek was rising because it had been raining up stream.

"Creek's up, Perry, creeks up!" I yelled back to Perry.

There wasn't time to wait and play, "I double dog dare you," with him because getting on over to the crossroads was the issue. So I double dog dared myself to jump the rising water without getting my britches legs wet. Needless to say, I lost my own dare.

I got both of my britches legs wet, and my poor brother got even wetter than I. Now, with a nicked jacket, and two little boys wet from a rising creek, it looked like it was going to be a tough day for this eight-year-old and his brother who had just turned eleven. As we made our way on across the pasture, we saw two bulls. The bulls were watching us as much as we were watching them. Since we were no threat to the flock, the bulls just observed us very closely with sad Miss Dolly eyes.

We crossed the fence on the other side of the pasture, and headed on toward the cross roads where we would usually meet the Mays kids. When I got to the cross roads, I was confused, and I tried to think while I waited for Perry to catch up because I thought we were late, and we were late. The Mays kids had already gone.

"How can we make up some time?" I asked Perry as we tried to keep warm.

We were getting further and further behind. To make up some time, we can go straight across, and go up that road where no one ever travels, I thought. And an answer came. No. Because over that hill is a swamp, and the swamp will surely devour you and your brother. Then I thought, maybe we can turn right and lead west toward the sunset while making our way over to the big road. And at the big road, maybe, we can hitch a ride. An answer came, No. No, because there is a rushing creek that lies between you and the big road, and you little boys cannot stand against its currents.

There we are, standing at a crossroad, and I don't know which way to turn. Oh, if only I could see my mother, she would surely tell me to just be still, and call on the name of Jesus. Jesus will tell you which way to turn. He will go with you, and he will fight for you. Then, I thought, I have the answer. We will just turn around and go back home. Then an answer came, "don't turn around now because the creek you just crossed is still rising. Instead, turn left and look to the east. Go toward the sunrise. Don't be afraid for I will go with you."

So we walked toward the sunrise. I would glance back and check on Perry at times. I was on the up side of the unimproved road as I approached a wooded area. I was trying to avoid a little stream of clear water that danced under a thin sheet of ice on the lower side of the road.

This uneven road caused me to get my pants soiled with red mud as I slipped and fell down to the lower side of the road. When I got to my feet, I checked on my brother who was on his way. As I kept on walking, the little stream of crystal clear water covered with a thin sheet of ice danced along. It crossed from one side of the road to the other; being pulled along by gravity. I was well entertained by the dancing water.

I was in a good spirit, even with my pants tarnished with red mud. Then I looked up, and when I looked up, my spirit was dashed. My spirit was dashed because I saw smoke, and I immediately realized that the smoke was coming from Miss Dolly's chimney. When I saw the smoke coming from Miss Dolly's chimney, I almost panicked. Then lead by a spirit, I was reassured not to be afraid, just keep on walking.

"I have greater things to show you while you are on this journey," the spirit called.

I can honestly say that I didn't see any one, I didn't know the spirit, but it knew me. So I turned my attention back to coaching Perry past miss Dolly's house. When I went back to see about Perry, he was in distress. I noticed he was leaning forward and shaking. My brother was freezing. He was crying and his nose was snotty. So I traced the tracks of his tears down past his lips and chin, and on to his jacket, and froze. I picked the frozen tears and snot off of his lips, chin, and jacket.

Then I said to him, "Perry, please hand me your books,"

He gave.

"Now, please give me your lunch,"

He hesitated, and then he gave me his lunch.

"Now, you can put both of your hands in your pockets, and it will help you keep warm." I told him.

Keeping warm that morning was a burden. Being eight years old, almost nine, I would have gladly accepted the opportunity to bear someone's burdens that day. Perry didn't know it, neither did I know that when he put the burden of his belongings on me and freed up his hands, that he was being prepared for a miracle that was about to happen.

The miracle was waiting to happen at the foot log. In my quest to make up time getting to school, I went on ahead of Perry to the foot log. When I looked back to check on him, he appeared ok. So I started on across, and when I got just past the half way mark of the foot log, I saw something that was very peculiar to the foot log. There suddenly appeared a shinny, crunchy patch of frost on the foot log. The patch of frost was about two feet long and the width of the foot log.

When I saw the frost, I held on to the drooping hand cable a little tighter with my right hand, while my left hand and my left under arm secured our belongings. When I had crossed the patch of frost and the remainder of the foot log, I turned right, and then I went back into the woods. That's when I heard a faint voice calling my name. I immediately threw ever thing down, books, tablets, and food, everything on the ground. It could have been an animal stalking, but nevertheless, I flew back to the foot log to check on my brother. Perry had contacted the patch of frost and slipped off of the foot log!And there he was, clinging to the hand cable, which was very slack, with both hands, water flowing fast beneath his feet.

"Pull yourself up, Perry! Pull yourself up!" I yelled.

My voice had no power. Then I ran off of the foot log and stumbled to my knees on the bank above the flowing water. And while I was down on my knees, I cried "Lord-help him to pull up, Lord-help him to pull up." When I cried Lord help him to pull up, Lord help him to pull up, I saw the results of Gods power come into my brother's body, and he struggled, and struggled, until, he was able to scramble and muscle himself back up to safety.

This single powerful act made me, at an early age, become a believer in the mysteries and the awesome works of God. Ever since I was eight years old, I've wanted to be a positive spokesman for my Lord. He gave me on that day, something to speak about. This was another miracle that I witnessed, resulting from living in the wilderness.

When my brother was okay, we went on to school and we had a positive day. But we still wondered about our mother's mysterious disappearance. And when we returned home, we returned to a joyous home. After the day had started so full of trouble, we learned that our mother was in the city at the hospital, and doing well. She was with child. February 12, 1950, turned out to be a glorious day,because that's the day my baby sister, Bonnie, was born.

7

Wilderness Occurrences, an Intercessor in the Field

The wilderness gave me a sense of purpose. I walked alone much of the time. Sharing whatever I had even when there wasn't much to share. I experienced much pain, and poured out my blood to near death. The wilderness experience also taught me the value of an intercessor because you can't always go it alone.

Speaking of hunger, well, I suppose when you are young; you don't have much tolerance for hunger. Especially when you have been at school all day and you have a more than two-mile rough journey to get home. Hunger did creep in at times; but the hungriest I have ever been was when my little school went on a field trip to the Grant Park Zoo in Atlanta, GA. We had walked more than two miles to school, boarded a bus, and traveled a little more than an hour to Atlanta. At the zoo, we had viewed many of the memorable attractions. Two of the memorable attractions were an elephant that had a great memory, and a gorilla named Tony. What was memorable about the elephant was his enormous statute and the way he got the hay he was eating into his mouth by way of his trunk. The elephant also had a very good memory.

We were told that he had remembered a man for ten years or so who gave him a chew of tobacco with his hay. The tobacco made him drunk. The elephant got even with the man the next time he saw him some ten years later. So we were told.

Tony the gorilla, on the other hand, was interesting because of his entertaining skills, and his crafted ability to get free food. Tony would sit right up front in his cage, and smile very broadly. Somehow, the crowds knew Tony liked peanuts, and he loved to clap his hands. When the crowds would say, "clap your hands, Tony," Tony would clap his hands and smile even more broadly. The crowds would then shower the gorilla with handfuls of freshly roasted peanuts, and he would eat. It was enough to make a little boy who had been active since early in the morning very hungry.

To curb our hunger, my mother had made my brother and me beautiful lunches. But our lunches did not appear so beautiful when it came time to eat. The hot sun had visited the bus where our lunches were stored and completely changed the appearance of my dear mother's beautifully crafted sandwiches. Everything was shiny with brown edges. My brother and I were ashamed to eat the food in the presence of the other children. We were hoping our chaperon would give us privacy and let us eat our food for we were very, very hungry. We didn't have any one to vouch for us because our sisters who were older, and who always looked after us, were with the older group of students. Our chaperon, not knowing how much we wanted our food, promptly threw our food in the trash. She wasn't trying to be spiteful. She just didn't know.

Now, here we were. We had to spend the rest of the day at the zoo, take an hour plus bus ride back to our school, and then walk more than two miles or so over rough terrain to get home. I was so hungry, weak, and so broken that I walked, and crawled on my hands and knees trying to get home. I cried a river into my heart that day. But again, it was a lesson; a lesson to be observant and to never ignore the needs around you. People are suffering all the time. Maybe someone was asking me, "will you be broken like bread to feed the hungry?" That river has never run dry, lacked the ability, desire, or the brokenness to feed the hungry that were within my reach.

I say, send me your masses. I will gladly give my last piece of bread, and say my last prayer to feed the masses for God. Yes, I'll be broken like bread and poured out like wine or blood upon the altar in the service of my Lord.

While I was living in the wilderness, I poured out my blood to near death two times. Both times, I was trying to be helpful to my family. The first time I poured out my blood, I was seven. I was cutting stove wood. When I struck the last piece of wood with the ax, the wood was partially cut and partially broken, and jagged. The piece of wood flew upward toward me, and the jagged end lodged in my flesh over my right eye near my temple. When the wood dislodged from my flesh, the blood came streaming down. It wouldn't stop,

The second time I poured out my blood out in the wilderness, I was nine years old; and I was hoeing corn with no shoes on. This was common. When my freshly sharpened hoe hit a large clod of hard dirt, the hoe skidded out of control, and thrust itself into the left side of my left foot. The impact of the hoe left a three-inch long and a quarter of an inch-deep gash in the left side of my left foot. The blood came pouring out. As my blood kept pouring out, it broke my heart. I was brokenhearted because I was trying to do my job and be helpful. Instead of being helpful, my family's whole flow of daily activities had been interrupted. We needed operational transportation quick to get medical help. We needed some strong wine to disinfect and cleanse the wound.

Since we had neither operational transportation nor strong wine, my life was in the hands of my loving but desperate family. They had to hurry and stop the gushing blood flow. Everyone looked to mother for a simple remedy. My mother had never seen one of her little ones bleed so freely and so heavily. She usually used soot, sugar, and spider webs to stop the blood flow from cuts and bruises. Some of my family members kept me hydrated and comfortable, while others were scraping soot from the fireplace and the lower part of the chimney. My mother managed to scrape up a little sugar. For some reason, she held the spider webs that day. Then my mother mixed the soot and sugar and made a simple remedy to stop the bleeding. My mother was a faithful genius.

The wound over my right eye and the wound to my left foot were treated in the same manner. Lovingly and miraculously, the innocent wounds have long been healed. Even though the innocent wounds have long been healed, the moderate scars yet remain. The scars may be laughable to some. The moderate scars always remind me of my toil, my suffering, my, wilderness existence. My mountains.

The weighty toil that I encountered in the fields out in the wilderness and elsewhere were the toiling grounds that my loving creator choose to give me my basic training for life in this uncertain world. He taught me through my mother and my family how to be honest, kind, compassionate, hardworking, how to get through losses, to follow his voice, and to be obedient.

He taught me about hunger, long suffering, pain, and brokenness. On his chosen training grounds, my awesome creator taught me another invaluable lesson. He taught me the value of an intercessor. I could not understand or comprehend the mystery, strength, value, and the saving power of someone praying for you.

One night, our oldest sister who lived in a faraway village showed up at our home unexpectedly. We suspected that she had walked the long distance alone because her husband was not with her. We did not see any sign of any vehicle arriving at or leaving our home. My sister was carrying a moderately sized bag, and her baby in her arms, and she was carrying a baby in her womb. No one was certain why she came. But she insisted that she urgently needed some time to be with the family. Just as remarkable was that she got up early the next morning, and went to the cotton field with us to pick cotton. I believe she went to the cotton field with us also to answer a call from the Holy Spirit that she had no knowledge of. My sister, Catherine, by being in the cotton field that morning, miraculously became my physical intercessor. The cotton field was glistening with fluffy white cotton. The cotton stalks were rich with large green unopened cotton bolls. The cotton rows were long and straight. The man whose field we were picking in had gotten far ahead of us children. Two of the children were the man's little girls. The little girls and I were all eight or nine years old. My sister just happened to be located between us children and the little girls' daddy. The little girls were not ready to pick cotton. They wanted to have fun instead. One of them thought it would be fun to throw cotton bolls. Cotton boll kisses! So she started throwing cotton boll kisses at me. Her sister encouraged her to keep on throwing them.

This was in the late 1940s or early 1950s when social behavior and racial relations were so very, very strained. I was not taking any part in it. And since I was not accepting her cotton boll kisses, the little girl appeared to have been getting frustrated. We had been commanded to get to pick the cotton that was before us. Everytime I would start to picking, I would get kissed again by another softly thrown, well placed, boll of cotton. So, in an effort to ease my frustration, I plucked a large firm green boll of cotton and lobbed it toward the little girl; it landed softly upon her shoulder. Now her frustration blew up. And when the energetic little friend of mine's frustration blew up, she threw off her pick sack; and she started running toward her daddy.

As she ran toward her daddy, she was screaming and crying, saying, "I'm going to tell my daddy you hit me. I'm going to tell my daddy you hit me."

Sister Catherine, an angel in the field. She had 8 children.

My oldest sister, who had traveled such a long distance, on hearing this, turned, and reached out her open arms. The little girl ran straight into my sister's out stretched arms. My sister caressed, consoled the little girl, and rubbed her rosy cheeks. My sister spoke kind and loving words to the little girl until she had no desire or need to tell her daddy that I hit her. My little friend meant me no harm. She was simply an innocent voice crying in the wilderness. She was screaming out a warning. A social warning while I was yet little. It was a lesson. Males shouldn't hit females, no matter what their age. Thanks Katherine, I am blessed that you were there for me. Thank God for you, love you endlessly.

If the little girl had told her daddy that I hit her, only God knows what would have happened. God proclaimed that the issue be resolved in the safest and the most wisdom inspired manner. Threfore, God sent my sister Catherine, an angel, who took control. Safety and wisdom prevailed. Angels do come to the fields. Judges 13:9, Luke 2:8–12.

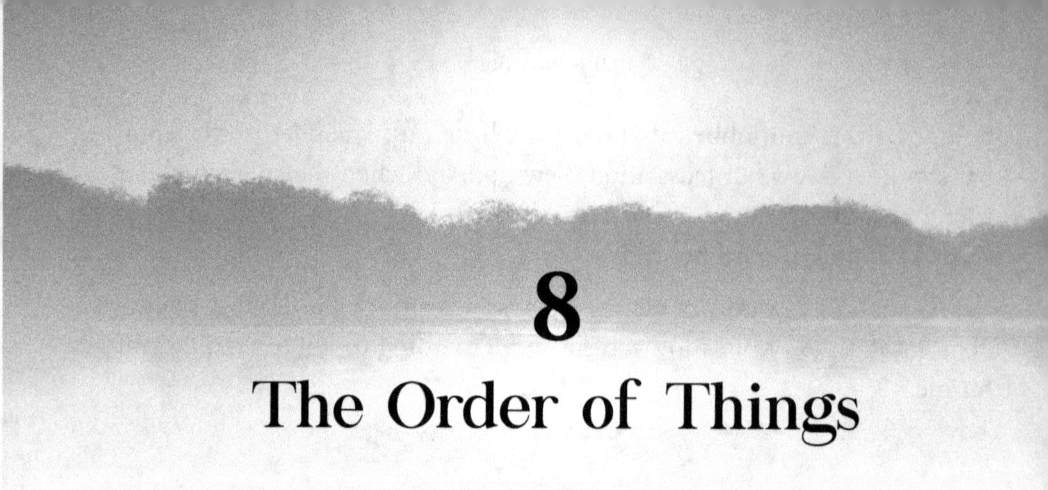

8
The Order of Things

I am confident that the wilderness living venture taught my family things, with each carrying a personal message, and personal value of its own; such as not being able to have visitation of the oldest child, my family had very few visits from anyone, having bouts with nature, issues of safety from beasts of the field, and things that crawled the earth. To live the real experience of "he taught us how." He taught us how to survive devastating family losses that would come later. We suffered the loss of our oldest brother who was the first-born to our parents. My family survived it, but my mother never quite got over the loss. We lost our dad. He died too soon, perhaps. But he worried. He worried because he was unable to provide for his family the way he'd like to. The sharecropper's life beat my dad. It beat him senseless. And after it beat him senseless, my dad's sharecropper existence slowly cheated him out of his life.

Then my younger brother Hubert mysteriously drowned while on a religious retreat. After awakening to all of these things and more, my parents suddenly realized that we had dwelled in a land for three years as farmers, and the land allotted to us to work was barren. It would not yield. The land would not yield sufficient harvests to support our basic survival needs. The three years we were out there in the wilderness, we planted various crops.

The first year we planted cotton. The second year we planted sweet bell peppers. The third year we planted various garden crops, except for turnip greens and sweet potatoes, the results were about the same, small yields. Perhaps, the small harvests were God's way of giving us rest and renewing our spirits. He strengthened and prepared our hearts to with stand the difficulties that only he knew we would face as we wandered along life's hard journey. We tried to build up the land. We tried to build up the land by nurturing it with tons of cow manure. And we even broke new ground for future use. After we had tried to build up the land and broke new ground, we found ourselves preparing to move again.

Where will daddy move us to this time? We hoped we would move to the city, but places to dwell in the city were scarce. So we couldn't move there. Therefore, my daddy's natural farming skills and educational woes landed us right back in the country. But that was well with us, we would have followed our daddy to the end of the earth. So we followed him back home to Stilesboro, Georgia, in the vicinity of where we so abruptly moved away from three years earlier. Moving back home had its blessings. We were blessed to meet our friends again when there was so much doubt if we would ever see them again. They were all the same, just a few years older. We were blessed that we could visit our friends almost any time without having to wait for the creeks to recede. We were able to play like children should play, and I even learned to play baseball. I also learned Christian drama, and played Joseph in the "Birth of Jesus" story during my last two years at Stilesboro elementary school. We enjoyed the convenience of the rolling store. We were able to walk to church and Sunday school regularly. Even though walking was our basic way of getting around, the environment for walking was much safer and much friendlier than walking in the wilderness. But there was yet that monster, that monster called sharecropping.

Since sharecropping was about the only work available to us then, it was a blessing to be away from the barren land that we drew to work in our last habitat. We were back at home where the soil was dark, fertile, and waiting to yield large harvests. But like anything else worthwhile having, there was a down side. The down side to getting the large harvests was, it took up much valuable school time. It was very difficult for sharecropper's children to get consistent school time to eke out a good education. I used to get so frustrated and ashamed when I would see some children on a school bus going in one direction to school; and I would be going in the opposite direction with my hoe over my shoulder, or my pick sack on my back going to the cotton field.

Some sharecropper's children easily missed three months out of a nine-month school year between planting, nurturing, and harvesting a crop. It took its toll during final exams. Many students walked into the final exam room, and seeing immediately that they were over matched, they left the exam room and never returned to school again. They became dropouts. We would be dropouts unless enough rain came where we could go to school instead of the fields. God's timing matched my prayer request for rain, and it came a long pouring rain. I thanked God for the favor. And I kept on thanking him for making it possible for me to get just one more day in school. So I pulled a clean pair of jeans from under my mattress that looked to have been pressed. I got cleaned up early in the morning, and I got dressed for school. But disappointment awaited me.

When my daddy saw me, he said, "good morning, son, where are you going all dressed up so early in the morning?"

"Good morning daddy," I said, with a glad heart and smiling. "I'm planning on going to school this morning because there came a pouring rain last night, and it rained a long time, daddy."

Daddy looked dejected.

Then he said, "well, son, it didn't rain long enough. I'm sorry, son. We have to go up in the high grounds and work. It will be dry enough to work up there by eight o'clock, eight thirty or so."

It broke my daddy's heart to say that, because he knew how much I loved school. It broke my heart as well.

"Work in the high grounds after all of that rain?" I asked my self quietly.

Working in the high grounds, after having been pumped to go to school, was like working on heartbreak hill. But daddy felt it was best to keep me out of school because he was looking ahead. He was looking ahead and thinking it would give him favor with the landlord, and the landlord would keep a roof over our heads another season. I stayed out of school that day. That's the day I learned how to hide my feelings, something that would actually benefit me later. I sealed my lips, except I wanted to say, "don't worry, daddy, I'll be right there beside you." I didn't wish to hurt my daddy's heart by complaining. A man trying to do well for his family is no reason to knock him, I conceded. And that's all my daddy ever wanted, was to do well for his family and pull us up.

To pull yourself up, you have to know the order of things. So I started watching for the order of things, and trying to discern just how life worked. I quickly learned that aside from God, in order to do well, one must almost always have an education. Every time daddy thought he was pulling his family up, the weight of the share cropper and the lightness of an education would pull him back down. We were doomed to go down with him. There was no mercy. No mercy because being a sharecropper, if that's all that you had, it was like playing a card game where the queen of diamonds was a player. You didn't play the queen of diamonds because she'd beat you if she was able.

She was able. She'd beat you at tallying up your books. She'd beat you at what went in your barn. She'd beat you until you were senseless. Then, she'd beat you because you had no sense. The queen of diamonds, the sharecropper's life, would beat you until your dear children dropped out of school. I certainly hope there never comes another de-energizing epidemic as we witnessed during the sharecropper era. And if it does happen, there should be laws, laws to ensure that all children get whatever it takes to get a competitive education and avoid the dropout syndrome. I believe that our great nation would be even greater, and the world would be better if this were so.

The iron-clad hands of the dropout syndrome had its chains wrapped all around me. But there was a hand on me that was stronger than the iron-clad hands. A voice kept on telling me to keep my mind on getting my high school diploma. "You can do something about it. It's all just a process," the voice kept telling me. So by seventh grade, I began to do something about it.

I started a self-assessment program to see how I was constructed. My self-assessment program labored on what effect would it have on my family if all of a sudden I were not there anymore.

I realized that we all worked together as a family, and we all depended heavily on each other. But, what if I weren't there? After all, I had worked diligently and produced quality work in everything God found for my hands to do out in the open country. It looked vain to me. It looked to me as if next year would be a repeat of last year So I started to look back at all I had done. I was humbled as I looked back. Not excited, but humbled. I humbled myself because of my health and strength. I was looking back to see what could be recalled and if I were on the right hill to leap in to God's destiny for me.

Here's what I recalled, I recalled that I had helped stuggling new born piglets and cleaned up. After their birth, I had learned to groom mules and follow the plow. I had shoveled and spread manure to enrich the land. I had hauled hay, and sacked wheat on a combine. I learned to prune fruit trees and pick their fruit. I sipped mellow honeydew from the heavenly honey suckle vine. I helped clean up newborn calves and puppies. I cleaned mortar from red bricks for a penny a brick. I could clean nine bricks a day, in the cold, when I was little.

I learned to pick cotton, and pull the pick sack up. But I could not discern if pulling the pick sack up was the total of God's will for me. Therefore, I needed to hunt for the answer. I desired to pull a hurting human being up instead of a pick sack. This desire burned inside of me. But getting this opportunity looked opportunity looked very unlikely while I was working out in the open country asa sharecropper. Who knows where the answer lies, and who knows what's best for a soul outside the will of God? Look again at the sharecropper. God gave them families, beautiful families; some with much happiness. By his own will, he let us toil with awesome labor, and he gave us sleep at night. And when the sharecropper could enjoy everything his fatigued hands had made, he found more rest, knowing this was truly a gift from God. Seeing how God provides for all of his people, should I now leave the open country and flee to a distant city where I have not a clue? Or should I let the process complete its course? But the process takes time; and then too, the process requires patience.

There is suffering during the process. Sometimes, the process breaks your heart. It just rocks you. So with much brokenness and much suffering, I choose with patience to let time dictate the will of God for me- as the dawn was yet breaking. After all, you can't run from every hurting situation. You are called to do God's will, and if you must stay out in the open country, then stay there. And while you're there, treat all the people you meet with kindness, because an angel might be among them. Angels do come to the fields. I conceived this notion again, when, at the end of the field where we moved too, a family moved in about forty yards from us. We got to know the family quickly, and we learned that the children from both of our families matched up closely in age. And being rural people, we were basically the same people. We were good people. We knew the same things, we talked about the same things, and we ate the same diets. We went to the fields early in the mornings where our feet got wet with the morning dew.

We toiled in the fields until late in the afternoons. We quenched our thirsts with the cool clear waters of the sandy-bottomed creeks. We cooled our hot, sweaty, and naked bodies in the deep still blue-watered swimming holes of the creeks that ran so freely through the countryside. We believed in our shadows. And we told time by the position of the sun in the sky... These were some of the distinguishing traits of rural people.

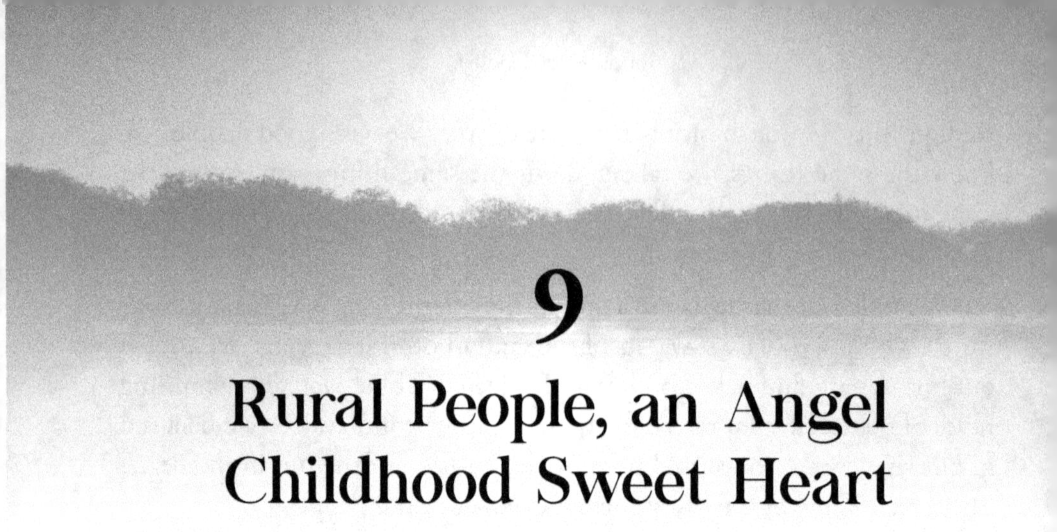

9

Rural People, an Angel Childhood Sweet Heart

Rural people were further distinguished as the same people because, as a rule, people out in the open country didn't possess an abundance of monetary wealth. But for the most part, we had our health. And it is much accepted that health is wealth. Since we didn't have an abundance of monetary wealth out in the open country, people were called to be thrifty with what little they had. So we learned to do without. You could resort to borrowing from your neighbors if necessary. A cup of flour, a cup of sugar, a package of cool aid, some Tetley tea, or a cup of corn meal, here and there. Families often became closely bonded by such graces. Many times when my mother would send me to our new neighbor's home to borrow an asset, a little girl, ten or eleven, about my age, would answer the door. And likewise, when the same little girl would come to our home to borrow, often times, I would answer the door. Being the same people and meeting out of necessity for the same identical cause, you might say, I met an angel.

The little girl who seemed to always answer the door became a symbol to me. She became like oxygen, essential to my life's processes. She was like the rose of Sharon; the rose, the most "perfect" of all flowers. She was even like the forbidden fruit of the Garden of Eden. She was simply off limits. As the sun shone upon us, day in and day out, we grew closer, but as we grew closer, we grew blinder. We were just innocent little children. Yet, by the time she was thirteen and I was fourteen, people began to notice similar traits in us.

Our similar traits were accented by kindness, loneliness, shyness, humility, and our head snapping fineness. People would often comment, "She is simply beautiful. And he is just as heart throbbing handsome. But their eyes are closed." It was comments like these that made us think that people were cheering for us to take the blinders off. We finally stopped, turned around, and opened our eyes. When we opened our eyes, we clung to what we saw. So we hurried and became best friends. As best friends, we became bonded. We were bonded like the ancient cement that bonds the tallest cathedrals together. We walked and talked together, and we labored many long hours on the same hot, sweaty farms. We pondered what would life be like after the farming life? Or would the farming life be our lot in life?

We tended the smaller children together. We worked in the consolidated school cafeteria together as friends. We were simply good friends. If one fell down, one could help the other up. We believed that if we were just one day away from destiny in the cold and the ashes were gray, and without heat, we could keep each other warm. But we were only dreaming. We were these two young children that no one had told that dreams are sometimes words of reverse warning of the heartaches to come.

Lingering heartaches did come. One day after my family had moved a short distance away, I got word that she needed to see me. When I arrived at her house that Saturday about mid- morning, she was home alone. And my friend was never at home alone. She was wearing a fresh summer dress. The fresh summer dress revealed her natural beauty, as she was having a morning snack. My friend's morning snack consisted of stewed apples in cow's milk.

"Want some?" She asked, as she reached the pint jar, and spoon that she was eating from to me.

"No, no, I thank you," I said politely.

There was a certain feeling about it all, and I didn't know what she was feeling.

Since I didn't know what she was feeling, I was a little uneasy. But our unbreakable childish bond, "if ever you need me, send for me," took away all of the jitters, and made my anxious heart bubble over to learn what was on her mind.

"I got your message!" I said excitedly.

She was silent for a moment. Yet love and kindness graced her beautiful face, as usual. But I could tell that something was not well with her. Her eyes told me so because stars usually danced in her heavenly brown eyes when we were together; but today, there were no stars. We maintained our dignity and our distance as we talked about it.

"I hope you're not upset with me for wanting to see you so urgently," she said. "But, it is about you. Well, it's about me too. It's about both of us," she continued.

I was thinking it was about us being too young to be as close as we were. But it was about another concern. I was concerned that the ones that had, had such endearing feelings about our, friendship, and the happiness that we shared were changing. Now the same ones; those very same ones, are trying to tear us apart; I imagined. Then she told me that it was about dating. She said that her daddy requested that she wait two more years until she reached sixteen, then she would be free to date.

10

Childhood Sweet Heart Break Up

It was bad news. And I felt so inadequate hearing this news. I knew that I heard her right.

But I was yet to ask her, "friend, did I hear you right? My dear friend, did I hear you right?"

The bad news hit hard. It felt like a walk off home run had just been hit against us. The ball game was suddenly and painfully over. Now it was all about character and obedience. To save our character, we had to play by the rules. So we swiftly obeyed. We thanked God that we had played by the rules, all the rules, including the no sex rule. There had been no sexual activity between us. Therefore, we believed we had glorified the Lord God, and our parents, that we had maintained our sexual purity.

Yes, we obeyed. But nevertheless, we were brokenhearted and crushed in spirit. Our lives, and activities were pure and just, we thought. We were only two lonely children who had learned to love and trust each other. And now, we were being suspended. Being suspended was like being put on pause. When two people love and trust each other, it is difficult to put that kind of relationship on pause for two years. But it wouldn't be forever, I reckon. Anyway, where would she be in two years? And where would life's circumstances lead me to in two years? Just think about the bonding; would the ancient cement and all the bonding hold any future for us? Or would it crumble and fade to loneliness and dreams? Would we ever pass this way again? These few questions lay in dreams; dreams sobbing for answers.

But sobbing dreams declined to deliver answers. Sobbing dreams only turned to mysteries that gave hope, and then hope slipped away. I dreamed of her in my arms at night, but when I awakened and tried to hold her, she had slipped away. She was gone. She had slipped away. She was… everything was gone it seemed.

Later on that summer, a man, Mr. John Willie, from one of the back plantations was out looking for workers to help him thin some corn that he had planted late. Early the next morning, he picked up members of my family and me first. As we stopped to pick up other workers, my friend was at one of the stops with her family and friends. Our eyes were cast upon one another. We were so surprised to see each other again. We spoke shyly, and then our eyes were immediately cut off from each other. We weren't talking, and even though, we weren't talking, the mere presence of each other tested our faith.

Here we were, we were getting too close again. The temptation was strong. They say it is good to run from temptation; but there was no place to run to for we were families and friends toiling in a cornfield. After about two hours of toiling in the cornfield in the presence of each other, the pain was getting deeper, and lingering longer. But God knows our troubles. He knows when we're hurting. God therefore devised a plan fitting for his exaltation and to reenforce our, serenity.

My creator sent the man who owned the fields to come and get me. The man was driving his well-maintained "B" model John Deere tractor. Now, this man was not one to let others drive his tractors, not even his oldest brother, Mr. Paul, who was among us.

The man said to me, "little boy, I have urgent business elsewhere. Will you take my tractor and plow behind the workers?"

I had never driven a John Deere tractor before. It was awkward, with the hand clutch, the power lift control on the rear, left side of the seat, and a single brake pedal on either side of the frame and all. Furthermore, I had never driven a tractor with a cultivator on it. The man showed me how to operate the tractor, and then he left. The other workers soon moved to another cornfield. I would have had to look back constantly to have seen them. And there was no looking back. This fifteen-year-old learned very quickly, that you cannot plow looking back. In order to not plow up the man's corn, my focus was strictly straight ahead and on the task at hand.

It was a test; God's timely intervention, and testing me in such a loving and mysterious way, spared my friend and me, our character. We no doubt glorified God once again by accepting sudden separation.

But this was the second occurrence of sudden separation for us. There must be a hand somewhere. There must be the divine hand between us, I thought. Then the spirit confirmed that we should just accept these two occurrences as a fact, that we had no control over. It was the will of God, and his will lay asleep within me. When I began to awaken, it was clear to me that she and I had been set apart. We were set apart, not for our own will and pleasure, but for God's holy will.

There came a revelation for me to give in to his will. When I gave in to God's will, my eyes were opened wide; and I realized that his blessings were fast upon me. I felt blessed that God had put her in my life in the days of my youth. It was about fate and all, it seemed. Before my fate was revealed to me, I had a (by chance) meeting with her, and God carefully placed certain somber words upon her youthful lips. Her youthful lips, startled, encouraged me forever with these few words, "*I feel safe in your presence.*" These few words, "*I feel safe in your presence,*" are heavenly words to me. I have since learned to tell Jesus these few words, "*Jesus, I feel safe in your presence.*" This blessing was a true and glorious gift from the Lord Jesus, who is my shepherd. Jesus has been my shepherd from the first day until this very day. He helped me through so many struggles. I knew that my struggle to be free together with my cherished childhood sweet heart would soon be over because the door to my heart was opened, and fate climbed in. My fate would lie in an unyielding but gentle spirit.

11

A Gentle Spirit Telling Me To Leave Home

The spirit kept on telling me to leave home. "Leave home, and come to a place set aside just for you." The spirit would plead with me kindly, yet persistently. The spirit always gave without taking. The spirit gave me visions of big beautiful fast trucks; and swift, powerful airplanes. It gave me dreams of my child hood sweet heart. The spirit didn't take away the love, the wisdom, or friendship of my queen of hearts, my dear mother from me. My mother knew all of her children's likes, dislikes, and concerns. She knew I was like unto self-assessments. My mother knew I would one day go away. So she talked to me. My mother talked to me with so much urgency and compassion that morning that it seemed as if she thought it would be her last opportunity. She was talking like the true Christian that she was. Mother knew that there wasn't time enough to restate everything she had taught me in my short sixteen years upon the earth. So she just reconfirmed the gifts of the spirit with me, "Love, joy, peace, patience, kindness, goodness, faithfulness, gentleness, and self-control."

Mother also talked to me about the unbreakable bond that existed in the spirit of the Lord between herself and me. She credited much of this bond to the careful timing of our birth dates.

"We were born in the same month, on the same calendar date, but thirty-six years apart," she said. "And while you were in my womb, I taught you every virtuous thing that you will need to know, to get through this world. If you stay close to the umbilical card that fed you, you will go places and do things that are uncommon to lowly people. And people will wonder how you got there. But people can't know how you got there. And they will look at you, and they will always wonder about you."

"Now here's your breakfast honey." Mother handed me some sugar biscuits. "Go ahead now, and take up your hoe and run on over to the field, and catch up with your daddy, and your brothers."

I walked outside and caught a glimpse of my daddy and my brothers far across the plain. I tried several times to go and catch up with them; but for some reason, I could not go. The people who often came to the field made me cautious.

After I kept getting pulled back, I went and told mother that, perhaps, I shouldn't go into the fields anymore. She was thinking it was about the hard work, and long hours.

"Mother, it's not about the hard work and long hours, I can do that. It's just a compelling thought that it would be more beneficial to the family if all of us children had the opportunity to be in school every day and not working in the fields."

"Mother, I know how important it is to the family, for me to stay out of school and help tend the farm. The farm can't wait and I know that. I'm getting so far behind in school, and school can't wait. Oh, can't they just saw me in two? I find no peace in the matter." So to find peace, I have made up mind to leave home." I said.

"Did you say you are going to leave home, my child?" mother asked, obviously shaken.

"Mother, I believe it's the right thing to do. I know daddy can't go to the landlord and report that he is releasing me so that I can go to school. If he did, he and the family would likely be put out of a place to live. So I have to bear my cross alone."

I struggled to hold back the pain as it over ran my eyes and trickled down my cheeks. Mother didn't get angry with me for wanting to leave. I think she knew that my leaving home, was the unavoidable result of divine will. She just told me how much my daddy was depending on me to help get the family moving in the right direction. But that awesome task fell to my, energetic brother, Perry.

"Well, Blackie, where will you go, my dear?" She asked.

Mother affectionately called me Blackie at times.

"I don't know, mother. I'm at a crossroad. Where can I go? I don't know where to turn, but I need to go somewhere, away from here. Where shall I go?"

"You are going to leave home and you haven't any idea of where you're going, my child?" Mother asked.

"I don't." I said regretfully.

Then I said, "well, mother, I'm thinking of going right down there, and taking to the highway. I can take highway 113 east, and hitch toward the sunrise. I can hitchhike the eleven miles or so up to Cartersville. If I can make it on a cross town safely, then I can pick up highway 41 and head south. With a little luck, I can hitch the forty-five to fifty miles on down to Atlanta."

"Atlanta? Did you say Atlanta? No, my dear baby, you are much too young and much too tender to be in Atlanta alone. Why, that would be the death of your daddy and me. Atlanta? No. Your mother is not going to approve of that. Your brothers, and sisters would not rest another day knowing that you are way down there in Atlanta wandering around by yourself."

They really tried to protect me through all of my trials. For some reason, I think they all loved me too much.

"There are so many trials." My mother said.

My mother knew the trials that I had endured would only mature me to a certain measure, but nothing like what I might face in a big city without guidance. My queen of hearts trembled at the thought of me living in Atlanta alone. She became weak. She needed encouragement, and she pleaded with the Lord for help.

"I declare Lord. God, please help me with this child of mine. Gird up my strength, and my unyielding love for him. Please join with me, Lord, to bear his burdens because this child cannot bear his burdens alone."

By now, my thoughts were getting so clouded. I thought maybe, I would stay, and don't go.

Then out of desperation, my mother said to me, "you stay here until I return."

My mother would not usually make a major decision without my daddy's approval. But that day, she went into another room and closed the door, and she started talking. I could hear her talking to someone, as if she was talking on the telephone. But there was no telephone in that room. When she came up out of that room, she looked more refreshed and more encouraged.

"Ralph Riley," she called with authority.

"Yes ma-am mother." I answered.

"I want you to go to school, and I want you go to Summer Hill high school in Cartersville. And don't you go one second past Cartersville."

Mother was never that abrupt with me, unless she was trying to head me off from a bad vision she had. Maybe an evil spirit could have been stalking. Now she's gentle again.

"And after school, Ralph Riley, go over to Courant Street, Someone will guide you. Go over to Courant Street and find your cousin, Bradley, and your cousin, Zadie Wyatt. I have been praying; and while I was down on my knees praying, I heard… I heard that Bradley and Zadie need help seeing after your aged grandmother, Ella Cooley, whose eyes are failing her. Your grandmother lives next door to Bradley and Zadie! Tell Bradley and Zadie that Horace and Ida Belle sent you up to them from the country. They will gladly take you in."

Then mother put some sugar biscuits and a change of clothes in a paper sack for me. Then I bade her good bye. When I left, she cried. In her tears, my mother reminded me to always take God along with me wherever I go and whatever I do.

"I will always be by your side." Mother told me.

Those words are with me till this day.

It was just me and my paper sack, and highway 113 north toward Cartersville. At Raccoon Creek, I turned and waved a last good bye to my mother who was standing in the front yard by the little brown house on the hill, above highway 113. I was tearfully/joyfully on my way to leaving home at age sixteen or seventeen. I had walked across the Raccoon Creek Bridge, up the hill, past the church and the cemetery, past the cow pastures, and the cotton fields. It's a long way from Stilesboro to

Cartersville, I thought as I kept on walking. If the tack in my shoe doesn't work loose again, I can make three more miles up to the country store, at the fork in the road. And at the country store, I can eat some of my sugar biscuits, I thought, as I kept on walking.

I had walked all the way up to a very dangerous curve in the highway, that curve that we called, "dead man's curve."

"It's a dark lonely journey when you are walking by yourself," I said, not talking to any one in particular.

"Oh, if the darkness of my loneliness would burst into direct rays of golden sun, it would blot out the darkness and rush in the everlasting light. I am out here on this highway hitching, where even the mere sound of a vehicle would be a symbol of light for me. Yet, I have seen and heard the sound of but a single vehicle. I've got my, strength, so I'll just keep on walking."

I kept on walking, and before long- I heard something.

When I looked back, I saw the biggest, fastest, and prettiest truck I know I had ever seen. And he was on full burn! As soon as I popped out my thumb, he started gear jamming, and backing it down, gear jamming, and backing it down, and he kept on backing it down; then he stood on his brakes. I hitched a ride with him. It seemed a little strange that the kind gentleman behind the wheel had never run highway 113 before.

And he reported that, "a woman, by the little brown house on the hill just before the creek, had a steady gaze in this direction. I felt that there might be a connection. So when I topped the hill back yonder by the Church, and the grave yard, I started hunting around for you."

He also said that he would not have anything to do with highway forty one or (lanna) Atlanta.

Then he stirred the coals and started gear jamming. He was still gear jamming when we approached the Etowah River. He had that big beautiful rig back on full burn as we crossed that mighty Etowah. He took me the most direct route to school. He let me out just a short walk up the hill from summer hill high school.

"Good bye, little boy. I'm glad I could get you off of that dangerous highway. Be kind to folks," he said.

"I thank you very much for the ride, sir, and I thank you for being out on the east bound highway today. And you do have a beautiful truck. Thanks, again, and have a nice day." I said.

I watched after the trucker as he started his take off roll. He shifted gears fast and, flawlessly. And he continued gear jamming as he disappeared into the distance. He had put distance between my loved ones and me. I felt sad to have left my family out there in the open country to carry on with the farming.

But it was a scheme given to me by a higher authority. Only God could send a big truck, and not a single car was out on the highway. I cannot phantom the path of the wind. I cannot conceive of how a body is formed in a mother's womb, so I won't question God's authority. Some people might discern that farming life is no way to raise a family. Farming life requires children to be out of school. I pondered all of these things as I walked the short distance up the hill to school.

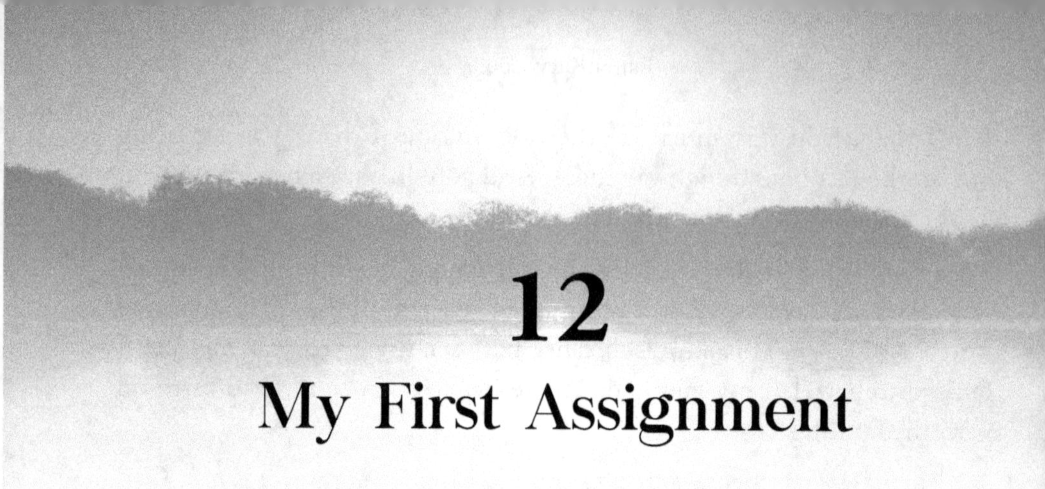

12

My First Assignment

There was a family in town called the Wyatts; their reputation was legendary. They were known for their kindness. People called them Mama Zadie and Daddy B. They were church people, you know, people you could trust. They were also avid supporters of the school and the school's football team. When I first met the Wyatt family, I found that they were every bit as nice as I had been told that they were. I introduced myself as Ralph Cooley, and then I told them exactly what my mother told me to tell them that, "Horace and Ida Belle sent me up to them from the country."

They recognized my name immediately. While they recognized my name, they didn't know if I were the same Ralph Cooley who had gotten injured in a football game last fall. When they learned that it was I, they took a sincere interest in me. They were saddened that they didn't come to my aid as I lay motionless on the football field. Mama Zadie and Daddy B accepted me right away after that. And then they introduced me to grandmother.

After I met grandmother, I was given some character expectations and what my duties would be. I was offered unyielding support to be in school every day. To earn a little spending money and to be responsible, I worked for Professor and Mrs. Morgan, my high school principal and his wife, an educator as well, for seventy-five cents an hour during school season. Grandmother and I got along great. We had the highest respect for each other. She got angry with me once only that I know of.

One evening when I came home from football practice, two teenage girls from the next street were visiting her. Grandmother became frightened because the girls showed me kindness. When the girls left, grandmother reminded me of what happened to Emit Till, an early teen. Both Emmitt and were fourteen years of age when he was so brutally murdered in Mississippi in 1955. Grandmother felt responsible for me, and I was not about to let her down. I am so grateful to grandmother, Daddy B, and Mama Zadie for so lovingly taking me in. I am thankful to my family for supporting me on this long, ambitious, and uncertain journey. And because of mother's prayers and God's provisions, ever thing happened just the way mother said it would. I was able to finish high school.

After high school, I desired to build a basic life of independence that would comfortably secure a family and help others just as I had been helped all my life. I wanted to help the masses. But the job market wasn't that promising, and financing for college was not even on the horizon. So I went to a US Army recruiter in Cartersville. I had high hopes of enlisting in the army. During an interview with the recruiter, I told him how much I loved this nation, and how proud I would be to serve.

I referenced my two brothers in law and others who were proudly and professionally serving our beautiful country, and how inspired I was with their newfound success. I also informed the recruiter of my strong desire to become a platoon leader, and that I would like to pursue that interest as far as time and miracles would allow. The army recruiter did the first steps of preparation for induction. Then he sent me for more interviews and testing at the military induction center in Atlanta.

After the interviews and testing were complete, the army recruiter handed me some heartbreaking news. They were not going to take me in the army. I sat there in silence. I restated how much I loved this nation and that I believed that my honorable service would be an asset to this country. I was disappointed and weary, not understanding the news. Not being taken into the army was the kind of news that could cause a soul to show weakness. To show weakness by trembling hands, teary eyes, and this was no time to show even a hint of that. But what could I do?

So here I am. No army, no job, and college was out of reach financially. And I can't show weakness? As I sat there and pondered all of these things, my Creator came in and commanded my youthful hands not to tremble—

and they obeyed. My Creator then praised my humble, stoic, and dry eyes while I counseled them not to dampen. Sometimes, you have to talk to yourself about yourself.

The U.S. Army recruiter noticed I didn't budge at the disappointing news. He smiled and said I was an excellent candidate for military service, but I was a better candidate for service in the US Air Force. Then he arose, shook my hand with concrete resolve, and escorted me down the hallway to a US Air Force recruiter. By the end of the day, I had been legally sworn in as a U.S. Air Force airman. This was a mystery to me. Although we don't always understand the meaning of a disappointment; sometimes, a disappointment works out for the best. I didn't know much about the air force because at the time, the US Air Force had only been an independent unit separate from the US Army Air Core for fourteen years. For some reason, this single event of being diverted into the Air Force virtually took me out of harm's way in Vietnam where so many young men lost their lives, and made so many mothers childless.

Should I have become a platoon leader in the army; I, being quietly courageous, at the hint of aggression, I would have declared, *here I am, send me. I'll bear the pain.* Even though I had boots on the ground in Vietnam on two or three short visit over time, I never had to bear that pain. I really wanted to be a platoon leader in the army, but it was not to be. Now that the swearing in had taken place, it would be a few days before my basic training would start.

The recruiters brought me back home to the open country to spend those few days with my paternal family. I wanted to spend those last few days with my paternal family because I sinned against them. I walked out on them just when they needed me most. At least that's how I viewed my actions. I heard about their awesome toil and how they suffered without me. But they didn't know how much pain and suffering I endured in making the decision to leave them. I needed to build a bridge over all the pain and suffering, and re-connect my family with the real me. Also, I wanted to ask forgiveness. Forgiveness for the inconvenience, hardship, and shame I caused my family because of my unkind, untimely, and secretive addiction.

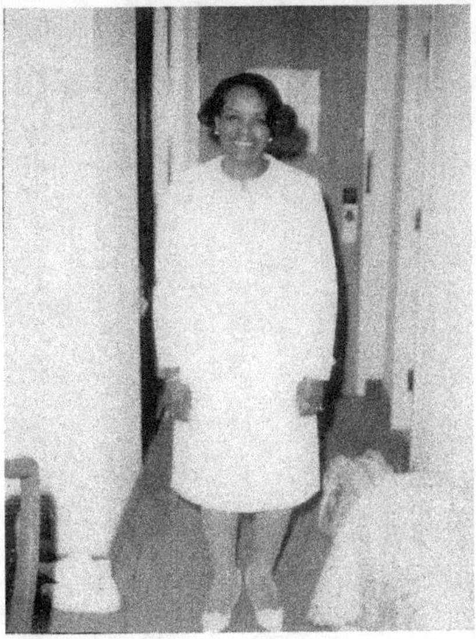

Sister Earlene, a true light to follow. She had 8 children.

No, I was not addicted to drugs, strong drink, wine, or cigarettes. I fell for a different and more expensive passion. I passionately was addicted to racing, drag racing. I had been drag racing ever since I was two, it seemed to me. The engine damage and other damages I inflicted on my family's cars was expensive, and there wasn't money for repairs. My sister's brand new car was also disabled because of me. I always wanted to apologize for any ill feelings or embarrassment I caused my family for my reckless actions. I had it right on the tip of my tongue. I was having trouble coming to terms with my selfish behavior, and I forgot to say I'm sorry. Today, though, some fifty-eight years later, I truly say I'm sorry. If God is willing, I shall repay.

My family welcomed me with open arms, then they handed me a hoe. Just like old times. It was almost August, and they were yet hoeing cotton in the blistering hot Georgia sun. The hot Georgia sun saw no colors; it just scorched every hint of your skin left uncovered. There was another family working alongside my family in the field. They were all good, kind, and friendly people. They didn't know me well since I had been away going to high school. They were curious, and they wanted to get to know me better. They wished me well on my military journey. I was glad to see the recruiters coming back to get me. When I saw them, I stood my hoe up in the earth, and bade everyone in the field good bye. We stopped at my family's house at the edge of the field, just long enough for me to get cleaned up and changed. My sister, Earlene, an army wife staying with my parents, offered me her bowling bag to use as a suitcase. I thankfully accepted. I filled it with a few things. I gave my last hugs, and kisses to the grown-ups and the babies, and then we were off.

13

Remembering the Early days And Basic Training

It was my family whose love and kindness and prayers got me through the toughest and most trying times of my formative years. I had been tossed and snared for so long. But now, there will be no more falling off the cotton filled wagon and getting my leg run over at age four. The days of having to go get the mules at six years old were gone, never to return. Again, when I was six, I'll never forget the day when that one and a half ton 1941 dodge came, took my family, me, and our belongings to include our mangy dog from our beloved home to go and live in the wilderness.

Going away to the military brought all my childhood events back to mind. While living in the wilderness, many adverse things happened. While I was cutting wood, a stick of wood that I was cutting flew up and lodged over my right eye when I was seven causing me to pour out my blood to near death. I remember finding our way to school, the poisonous snakes, meeting Miss Dolly, seeing the mysterious patch of frost on the foot log, and my brother dangling over the water after slipping on the frozen patch. All this before I was nine years old. At age nine, I split my foot open, again pouring out my blood to near death. I remember cleaning red bricks for a penny a brick, sipping the mellow honey dew from the heavenly honey suckle vine, and the John Deere tractor that plowed between my childhood sweet heart and me. I remember leaving my dear mother praying and crying when I left home at age sixteen. And the big beautiful truck that so mysteriously and conveniently lifted me up to safety from that lonely east bound highway. Oh, if I could discern the meaning of things.

I'll remember the John Deere tractor plowing between my childhood sweetheart and me. When I look back, and I will surely look, back, I'll always remember graduation day. My parents and my siblings will be forever remembered. Likewise, Mamma Zadie, Daddy B, grandmother, professor, Mrs. Morgan and family, and the Carson family were very dear to me. The Deans, the Peeks, the Hendricks, the Banks, the McClendon family, the Henderson family, and so many others were also dear friends of mine. I'll remember my teachers, my football coaches, and my beloved football teammates.

I'll remember my beloved and honorable (child hood sweet heart,) Bobbie. Bobbie was beautiful, pleasant, and a truly wise friend. She forever blessed me with these unforgettable few words, "I feel safe in your presence." I'll also remember my amazing (high school sweet heart,) Vivian. Viv had a heart of gold, a sparkling sense of humor, and she was kind. She was beautiful, beloved, and she was highly respected. Above all, Viv was a trusted, true, and a godly friend of mine.

With all of these events, blessings, and friendships tightly stitched inside me, how could I say good-bye? But it was now time to do just that. If you really think about it, you can't fully say good-bye when your only fabric is stitched to your loved ones. It was like having your umbilical card cut all over again. It hurt. And it hurt even more to know that only by fate would I ever see them again. You can't wholly say good-bye to the ones who love you. It was love that made me yearn to return with provisions and shower the masses with blessings over flowing. But, in the meantime though, I'd be on the move to where ever in the world that had been predetermined for me to go. I prayed that many blessings would overtake my loved ones and me. Blessings that are as assured as the tide ebbs and flows twice in twenty- four hours.

I was soon on a jet plane heading out of Atlanta to basic training at Lackland Air Force Base near San Antonio, Texas. Our flight to San Antonio originated up north. When the flight arrived in Atlanta; it was hyped with northern recruits. When we, southerners came, aboard, our flight became even more charged. The reason things got more turned up was that the northerners brought up the civil war. We stayed awake all night as we storied the civil war all the way to San Antonio. And the South did rise again.

As soon as we realized that we were about to begin basic training, the northern recruits and the southern recruits rose together as one. We rose together as one nation. Basic training was an interesting experience; everything that we did was for one nation. All phases of basic training almost always returned to be an asset as time marched on throughout my career of a quarter of a century. The precision marching, the strict discipline in the dining halls, the academic training the survival training, the physical training, the strict attentive caring, and looking after your fellow airmen were vitally important. I believe our training instructor (TI) had a type of psychological training discipline to quietly drill into our young, homesick souls.

There was discipline in a song. The song that seemed to have always been playing when we marched past that small open-air café was, *Rain Drops*.

Raindrops, it feels like rain drops falling from my eyes. Since my love has left me, I'm so all alone. I would bring her back to me, but I don't know where she's gone. Rain drops, so many raindrops, they keep on falling, falling from my eyes.

That song spoke volumes. It strengthened and it weakened at the same time. Basic training was also a place where if you had a weakness or weaknesses they would be exposed, and you needed to spin any frailties into strengths. Nothing else will do in a time of war. If you couldn't make such a transformation from weakness to strength, an early ticket back home was on your schedule. But, I simply said, "if my Creator is willing, He will gird me up with strength and dignity, so I could stay, and prepare to serve this great nation of ours." So I worked courageously, and when you're working with a purpose and trying to do what is good and what is right, you always attract a competitor, it seems like to me.

My competitor's antics started with marching. There usually wasn't anything to gain from our marching positions. My marching position was third man in the first squad. My competitors' marching position was third man in the second squad. The marching positions alone made us incredibly equal in statute. Maybe he wanted to march taller than I, but why? My marching skills were ordinarily not something to be modeled.

One day when our TI was encouraging and motivating us to march even taller and with more precision, I got so encouraged and so motivated that my marching skills stood out above all the rest. So much so-that I immediately secured a position of importance in marching. I was elevated to the position of right guide. The right guide is responsible for the direction and cadence of the march; and he is the leader for the entire flight.

Now that the marching issue was settled, the concern and competitiveness spilled over to the athletic fields, obstacle courses, the academics, physical training, and field training. I was competent and comfortable with my unit, yet there was no light. I, being a self-proclaimed introvert and loner, was simply uncomfortable with the unsolicited competition. I thought the unsolicited competition was meant for evil; but God, my Creator, meant it for good. My creator, with his all-knowing and all seeing infinite wisdom, knew ahead of time that if I continued to be the introverted loner that I was, my light would be suppressed. Therefore, my heavenly father raised up this young, ambitious, contemporary, and someone of my own standing to shadow me and to push me out of the shadows. Consequently, the day came that I was found lacking and it brought an emergency along with it.

We were locked up in a small window of time as we prepared to go swimming. We had just returned to the barracks from field training. In that small window of time, we were required to change from our utility uniforms into our physical training (PT) uniforms which included the utility cap. Plus, we were required to leave the barracks in full inspection order. We were all working with a great sense of urgency to meet the time constraint and other requirements. Then came the order to wear our pith helmets, a light sunhat.

While reaching for my pith helmet and trying to get to my post ahead of everyone else to align the flight, I totally slipped my utility cap. I knew it as soon as I left the building. I hoped there would be no inspection, but we were inspected at the swimming pool. Our TI used my situation as a fruitful training session for the entire flight. After he talked to (chewed on) the entire flight, he sent me back to get my utility cap. It was about one half mile from the swimming pool to the barracks and back. It was a worrisome half-mile. "How could I have let them down?" I asked myself. I felt like I had let the whole world down because I made a mistake.

I was determined not to duplicate my mistake by being slow to return. So I broke into a quick sprint. The quick sprint turned into all out running. I ran as fast as my sleek linebacker legs would carry me. I did not realize that the intense heat might become a factor. Then I suddenly started to feel the burden of the rays, drops of golden hot Texas sun, but I kept on running. When I returned to poolside with my utility cap properly fitted under my pith helmet, I got inspected again, and I entered the water almost immediately after the inspection.

As soon as I entered the deep end of the pool, something went helplessly wrong. My body became locked up in pain and I was totally powerless to break free. The mighty spasms to my legs and abdomen made it difficult to maintain my position above the water.

When I regained consciousness, my rival, my competitor, was right there saying, "I saved your life. I was able to save your life because I know you better than anyone else here. When I saw that you were not able to fight for your self, I immediately came down, and lifted you up to safety."

I thanked him with all the grace my heavenly father handed me. It was for God's glory and my growth. I continued on through basic training while learning and growing. I leaned on strict adherence to the doctrines that were so ever valuable to life and to the objectives of the US Air Force.

I successfully completed basic training without a single set back and only one, maybe two demerits. I appreciated the strict discipline. The strict discipline was a complimentary reinforcement to how I had been raised all of my life. Now that basic was about over, I received my first assignment. I was assigned to Seymour Johnson Air Force Base in Goldsboro, North Carolina.

I went home on a few days leave after basic training. I had written my dear mother a few days ahead of time and asked her to please prepare for me a place to rest. I truly needed a place to rest because I was exceeding tired. My dear mother made our home comfortable for me. After getting some rest and visiting people, it was time to catch a grey hound bus. I sat by the window on the grey hound as I made my way from the city of Cartersville, Georgia up to Goldsboro, North Carolina to start my first real assignment. There were many starts and stops along the way.

The gate announcers were entertaining as we went from station to station. Also from station to station, it was interesting to see the directional signs on water fountains, bathroom doors, and other public places. There were lots of little children boarding the busses, their mothers lifting them up by their wings as they climbed the steep stairs on the bus. I was confident that we would make our destinations safely, but only God knew what was ahead.

14
Assignments

With the baggage and all the troops loaded, about two hundred in all, it was time to taxi a very heavily loaded, DC-8 four-engine airplane.

We held short of the active runway while several fighter jets took off. The fighters would use the minimum of the runway. Then, they would nose up in a near vertical posture, hit the after burner to gain more power, and they would jump on up into the atmosphere. They showed a real sense of urgency.

The sense of urgency was to protect against enemy ground fire. The policy for takeoff at Ton Son N-hut air base was to climb to at least six thousand feet as quickly as possible after takeoff. Now, with the fighter jets securely air borne, it was time for us to try. As we started our take off roll, TSgt Baker, realizing that the fighter jets were lighter than we were, commented that he hoped that we could lift up over that fire and smoke over in the distance in time. When we thought we had successfully cleared the fire and smoke, we heard a thump on the left wing of our airplane. We had taken a hit from ground fire, I recon.

As soon as we came out over the South China Sea, the pilot came on the intercom and he very calmly stated, "gentlemen, there is no need to panic, but I'm going to have to feather number one engine."

No sooner than he said feather, he stopped the engine.

"We'd be a setting duck trying to get back to where we just left."

There was a strong wind coming out of Thailand against us, a jet stream.

"With just three engines and being heavily loaded, we simply could not run against the wind. We frantically needed to land the airplane."

We had no land to land on. The only thing left to do was to put our back side to the wind, and kindly ask the wind, the jet stream, to push us along to Clark Air Force Base in the Philippine Islands, but that sounded risky. Because things seemed risky, that whole airplane became a somber sight to behold. There was the look of people praying. Quiet sobs came from some of the sharp shooters and marksmen who had been away from home for a year, and some had hankies over their face trying to hide the tears. Bake, my traveling partner, was beside himself.

Bake was upset because he had been away from home about six months, and he feared that he would never see his family again. He was so upset that he pulled a perfumed letter from his shirt pocket with pictures of his family and vied them. He let me see his two children, his family pet, a black curly haired poodle, and his wife. Then he made some heartfelt remarks about his family. Bake, then, looked again at his children, and he looked again at the family pet. Then he took a long and affectionate look at his charming wife. Then, he savored the aroma of her perfume upon the letter. I had some similar tokens of remembrance of my family as well.

We were strong men; but the general mood was we had no control. We felt that we were going to crash and drown in the South China Sea. There was the true reality of having no control, and there was a strong feeling of helplessness among the passengers. So I told Bake that I can't face it. Then I jockeyed around in my middle seat until I found a resting place. I said a prayer, I felt safe in Jesus' arms; and because I felt safe in Jesus' presence, I closed my eyes to rest. Because it appeared that there was no way out, I rested peacefully for a long time and then all of a sudden, I felt sharp blows to my left side. It was Bake elbowing me.

He was saying, "wake up, Spade. You're not going to sleep. You're going to face it just like the rest of us. So wake up, Spade."

Note: Some people called me "Spade" in honor of the great "Spade" Cooley, an accomplished guitar player. Some people called me "Spade" because the hot South East Asian sun had baked me to be as black as an ace of spades. Anyway, the reason Bake was saying, "you're going to face it just like the rest of us," was because our number two engine was trying to quit. This would have put both engines out of commission on the left side of the heavily loaded airplane; and because of this, Bake was convinced that we were not going to make it.

The number two engine had begun to backfire and sputter. The engine would backfire and sputter, backfire and sputter. Bake was convinced that we were going to crash into the sea. The number two engine, which was trying to bear up under the load, would backfire and sputter. Every time the engine would backfire and sputter we would lose altitude. The sea waves were high and bright with foam. There wasn't much time to pray, but I remembered that my mother told me many times, "if I ever need to pray and there wasn't much time to just say, 'Lord have mercy.'"

Sister-In-Law Vernell, my mother Ida Belle a divine matriarch, and me, Ralph Riley Cooley.

Every time the engine would back fire and sputter, and we were losing more and more altitude, I would say, "Lord have mercy, on us." My family must have been praying a very different prayer. My mother must have been praying, "Lord, build a bridge. Please build a bridge, Lord, because my child and all of those men are somewhere over troubled water." As far as you could see, there was nothing but troubled water. Even a man of faith has thoughts of doubt in times like these. But let me back up a bit and start from land long before we ever took that fateful flight.

It was early October 1961. At Seymour Johnson, I served with the 4th Tactical Fighter Wing of the Tactical Air Command (TAC); the 68th Bombardment Wing of the Strategic Air Command (SAC), and the 482nd

Fighter Interceptor Squadron (FIS). In this environment, life was about careful living and intense learning, in that order. I was assigned to the dormitory. Both of my roommates were from Philadelphia, Pennsylvania (Philly). They're names were, Raymond Crooms, my look alike, and Benjamin Richardson (Big Ben). Ray, Big Ben, and I were found to be in harmony with each other. It was paramount to be in harmony with one another. We were working around powerful, jet-propelled engine aircraft. In that environment, arguments and dissention just don't work. We worked with equipment in the aerospace fuels laboratory such as the analytical balance that was so sensitive that you could weigh your fingerprint on it.

As I progressed in my training and received my security clearance, I was permanently assigned to the flight line. After observing and learning the orderly patterns of aircraft associated equipment and aircraft disciplines, I acquired a strong desire to be more a part of aircraft operations. I actually longed to fly. The two aircraft I was most attracted to were the F4 phantom fighter jet, a frequent transit to Seymour, and the B-52 bomber jet, the Stratofortress. While I acquired the desire to fly, I did not take into consideration that I may have already had my wings clipped and was already grounded.

But nevertheless, I admired the F4 for its strength, its weapons system, and its world record zoom climb (F4H-1) of 98,557 feet on December 6, 1959. The F4 modified also achieved an absolute speed record of 1,606.342 miles per hour on December 22, 1961. I was attracted to the B-52 for its weapons systems, its representation of power and deterrence, its eight J57 engines, its impressive 185-foot wingspan, and it's incredibly huge fuel capacity. Following certain missions of nuclear deterrence, we would often push the B-52s up to 301,000 pounds of jet fuel to quench their thirst. Sometimes, it would take as much as 42,000 gallons of fuel to bring them up to the required 301 thousand pounds. The B-52 was also air to air refueling capable in case you ran low on fuel.

I also choose the B-52 because it could release such an arsenal of weapons from its bomb bay. Some of our adversaries referred to it as raining steel or steel rain. It is important to note that this nation's awesome air power is not just for death and destruction, but more for the deterrence of death and destruction. The B-52 was a champion in the Mutually Assured Destruction (MAD) phase of the cold war.

As I observed more and more the sources of our mighty air power, I investigated into it to see what my possibilities of flying might be. My investigations revealed that I had indeed had my wings clipped and I was already grounded. My wings were clipped and I was grounded way back in grade school when the cotton fields outbid the schoolhouse for my attendance.

Let me digress for a moment and talk about school attendance. Some children and I could hardly see a day in school before thanks giving, but some children, many children, before they are born, were destined to barely ever miss a day of class. These children will never have to miss one hour out of school unless it's for sickness or some other miss fortune. By third grade, there is already planning for advanced degrees for some. Do not envy them. Be glad for them. Be glad for yourselves as well, because if the laws are right, I believe a child in contention with a job over school. I believe school will win for that child.

But then, be ye wise about it and just say, "Lord, do with me what you will. I'll always be here to serve you in what- ever capacity you have chosen for me." But don't be a drop out just because it is your will. Stay in school if you can, get a good early education, and then build on it. Because you never know what opportunity you may have later. Thrive in school and be prepared to leap into whatever God's plan is for your life.

Maybe flying was not in God's plan for me because it would have taken a huge amount of education and training in addition to what I needed to have become a jet jock. My will insisted that I could have become a superior jet pilot. I think I lost another little piece of my heart for not jockeying for it. But then, the air force has such high standards. To fly takes a high level of skill. You can only go after a target twice because the gas is so much you can't go by three times. The overall standards were so extreme, but so appropriate. Any job you are assigned, even outside the cockpit, rings with integrity. With this in mind, I conceded that the jet jock romance was just an illusion. I let it go. I Just let it go! I continued to work as hard as I could to become the best aircraft ground support airman I could be. Then I went on with my life. Going on with my life, I guess, meant having some kind of a sensible social life.

My social life began around Christmas 1961 when a dormitory friend of mine voluntarily made a blind date for me. I was leery of blind dates, painfully leery. So I told my friend that I was okay staying in the dorm as usual. Then it became a character issue. My friend was certain that I would defame his character if I stood the young lady up. So I went along with his human kindness. As a result of the blind date, I met a wonderful local young lady. Her name was Barbara Jean Chestnut.

After about two months of our acquaintance, we started making wedding plans. Our desired date for getting married was June 1962, but this date hinged on whether I got promoted during the June promotion cycle for pay purposes. I was scheduled to make E-3 in June. Should I have made E-3 in June, it would have increased my pay by sixteen dollars a month. My current pay as an E-2 per month was $108.00. I was having a fifty-dollar savings bond deducted from the $108.00 monthly award. But of course, my shared dormitory room, and dining hall meals were free. But earning such a small amount of money—the whole marriage notion had to have been about humility, hope for continued love, and for prosperity. Only marriage can temporarily suspend a person's logic. So many people are perfectly fine getting married without money, all the while knowing it takes tons of it to survive. I guess I was one of them. I didn't get promoted in June. But surely I'd be promoted to E-3 during the October 1962 promotion cycle. Thankfully, I was.

October showed up. I had gotten promoted. All we needed now was to take our wedding vows. But when I checked the status of my leave request, I found that a hold had been placed on my leave. My judgment, by just watching the mood of things, told me not to probe too much because everybody's lips were sealed for some reason. When things started to loosen up, I learned that I, along with many others, had been targeted to go on red alert. We were being put on red alert to go and help with the Cuban Nuclear missile crisis, the world's worst potentially deadly crisis.

At times during the crisis, the United States and Russia were within seconds of completely destroying each other under the Doctrine of Mutually Assured Destruction (MAD). But President John F. Kennedy and Soviet Premier Nikita Khrushchev negotiated a truce that averted disaster. Now with things virtually back to status quo, some people's duty was returned to normal; and my future bride and I went with our wedding plans in late October 1962. Our first year of marriage was tough on us.

Son Carl on Prom night.
Occupation: WEB analyst.

Brother Perry, a faithful gospel preacher and his wife Emma Jean Cooley

Sister in law Dianne, a faithful servant of God.

My brother Hubert on the left and his Air Force friend on the right.

Brother Carey, a great guy whos after God's own heart.

Son Reggie, Berkley School of Music student. Jamal's Dad.

Monica Ward, the daughter we never had.

Grand Son Jamal and Grandma Barbara Cooley.
Jamal's motto: to woo the worlds people thru music.

Barbara and friends, Nita Rice and Sandra.

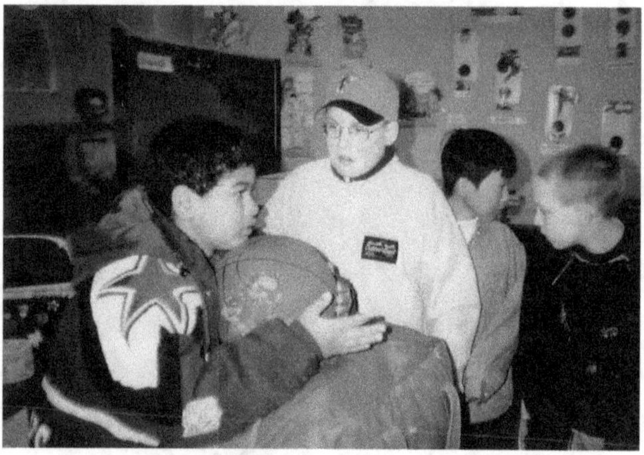

Grandson Jamal, Brian Rogers and friends.

Janet Cooley, mother of our only grand child, Jamal.

15
Getting Married

We had meager beginnings. We lived in the projects in Goldsboro. I often volunteered for kitchen patrol duty (KP), scrubbing pots and pans, peeling potatoes, and mopping the dining hall floor to help pay the rent. We had no car. So to help with transportation matters, we bought a brand new three-speed red and white western flyer bicycle for about fifty-nine dollars on credit.

Ralph and Barbara's wedding, Age 21. Oct. 1962

Credit/debt, this was our first mistake. But anyway, we made do with the bike until the harsh winter weather made it unsafe to ride the bike to work. Then we bought our first car. We got a great deal on a two-tone gray 1950 Chevrolet standard shift. It was a little faded and it needed only a starter.

A fellow airman, Granger, let us have the little Chevy for just eighty-nine dollars. That's all we could nickel up. Despite the starter trouble, the little gray car ran pretty well after pushing it off to get it started. Barbara, my wife, helped a lot as she was working; and I got a part time job. Then, we were able to juggle the rigors of military life, parenting, and traveling.

Time marched on as I continued my training and my work with the powerful aircraft. I continued working, helping get the SAC aircraft serviced, and ready for missions of deterrence in support of the cold war. Everything was well with the air force. I tried always to be on good behavior. Because of good behavior and excellent job performance, I was sent to other bases on temporary duty (TDY) at times. I would always return to Seymour for duty, and everything was well with my family and me.

We were doing so well, in fact, that by February 1965, I had gotten promoted to E-4. I had re-enlisted and we had bought a new car. My family and I were in upward transition, and we were so very thankful to have been shown such favor from heaven. But almost in the same breath of the upward transition, the clock stopped for an instant. The clock stopped because things were heating up in Vietnam, and I received orders to Southeast Asia.

By April 1965, in the wake of the war in Vietnam, I would report to duty at Seymour Johnson Air Force Base for the last time. The last time ever. By May 1965, I would say good-bye to my lovely wife and our two sons for one year. Leaving home and going to the far corners of the world to help keep peace in the world and help preserve the sovereignty of America the beautiful, was a matter of ordination. That's what some great military leaders will tell you. You have to be ordained for military service. Bearing the feeling that I was so ordained, I was able to go on.

But sometimes, it pierces because a man is also ordained to care for his family. My wife and I were just establishing roots in the community as a family, and we were bonding with society. That would be interrupted, and that pierced me deep. I had made a union with someone with whom I had planned to grow and keep that union for a lifetime. I was about to lose one whole year of that union, and that pierced me deeper. But being young and faced without enough funds to care for my family from a distance was the fourth and deepest piercing. My wife and I knew right away that this would require two budgets. One of them would have just enough money and one budget would have not quite enough. The latter fell to me. My wife would inherit the responsibilities of managing the family in my absence. I hoped that the new car would be a blessing to her and others who needed a lift getting around town and to church. With the budgets settled and leave time flying by, soon I would be on my way.

The flight from Raleigh-Durham to San Francisco was lonely. Tonight would be lonely. Tomorrow would be lonely. And the following 365 days would be much the same; but I'm ordained, remember?

At San Francisco airport, we were greeted by six or seven-year old children and their keepers. The little children were aware that the military were departing for Vietnam in Southeast Asia, and possibly into harm's way.

So they showed much kindness and concern for our safe return home. The children showed concern by singing songs of encouragement, compassion, and hope. But also, they were asking for donations for charity as well. At first, I gave little; I gave according to the little that I had. Tomorrow, I'll have little; and 365 days hence, I'll still have little. At boarding time, the little children were yet singing, and reassuring us that their singing would help bring us back home alive. The thought of coming home alive, being manifest by little children, gave me more incentive to give. Then I dug deep into my meager cash on hand and I gave more freely. We thanked the babies and their keepers and then we boarded the aircraft for the first leg of our long trip across the spacious Pacific Ocean. In time, we arrived at Hickam Air Force Base Hawaii where we met with more kindness, but there wasn't much time to tarry at Hickam. Our flight carried us over the halfway point of the pacific over Australia and the International dateline (IDL).

When we were approaching the IDL at about midnight, a flight attendant unexpectedly announced for us to put our hats on and turn them backwards. There was not much response to this request at first as some were sleeping. But as soon as she repeated the request and adding, "by turning your hats on backwards as we cross the (IDL), this symbolizes that you will come back home alive," the request was then happily and heavily responded to.

As soon as we had crossed the (IDL), we lost a full day, twenty-four hours. It didn't matter though because we were assured of regaining the time, as we would travel back westward toward home a year later. We continued on Eastward towards Wake Island and the Philippine Islands. We made a refueling stop at Wake Island, a small atoll managed by the US Air Force.

They got us refueled in the minimum of time. We lifted up off of Wake just as the dawn was breaking and continued on our next leg toward the war zone. But mind you, we had one more important stop to make. The next stop was important for two reasons. Reason one, was because the crew needed to rest; and reason two, was because us GI's needed to get qualified on the powerful M-16 assault rifle.

These two disciplines were scheduled to take place at the very busy Clark Air Force Base in the Philippine Islands according to our itinerary. Our itinerary was well thought out and a good one if everything was to go according to schedule. When we landed at Clark, we left our major luggage on the aircraft. The crew went on crew rest, and us, GIs, prepared to go to the firing range. We were scheduled to meet our flight crew at some point after things got done and fly on to Tan Son Nhut Air Base, Vietnam on the same airplane. But could we get it done? The host tried frantically to keep us on schedule because they didn't want to see us miss our original flight and have to resume our travel on a noisy C130, or spend a lot of time in the over flowing transit huts.

No, we could not get it done because after all, this was the first big buildup of the Vietnam War. Consequently, the firing range was teeming with Vietnambound troops seeking qualification on the M-16. Therefore, we missed our original flight. We stayed over for maybe a couple of nights. And we stayed in little huts that the host had set up to help handle the over flow crowds.

The little huts were fitted with screen wire that came down about three feet from the top, and a screen door for ventilation. From about the three-foot mark down, there was privacy. Well, you had privacy if you didn't count the native lizards. They were called blank you lizards by some who had encountered them. Those little green lizards would get on the screens and try to run you out of town, it seemed like to me they were constantly saying, blank you, blank you, blank you, blank you, blank you.

The lizards were harmless though. When you're dizzy from fatigue and travel beaten, you just kick off your tired shoes and try to get some rest. You appreciate that God wired the lizards the way he did. They were there to protect us from other pests, such as insects. We were more concerned about getting on the firing range, so we could move to South Vietnam and the battle zone anyway. When we finally got qualified on the M-16, there was a flight and a flight crew ready. Sure enough, we'd be flying on a C130. I think it was an "A"-model C130 because the engines were very loud. Typical of the T56-A-9 and the T56-A-11 turbo prop engines associated with the "A"-model Charlie 130s. They were known to be much louder than the T56-A-7 engines on the "B" models and later modifications of the C130s. Now, despite the loud engines, we were ready to travel.

16
Traveling to Vietnam/Thailand

With just our carryon luggage, about a third of our original passengers, and with our backs to the walls of the C130; we strapped ourselves into the red webbed seats. Then we departed Clark Field and headed out over the South China Sea, toward Tan Son Nhut Air Base, the gateway to South Vietnam. The noise of the T56-A-9s or 11s was loud and relentless. But it was a sweet, loud, positive noise because the engines sounded strong and they showed no sign of stopping. There was no good reason to be stopping now because I had done a lot of traveling. My tenure had taken me from Goldsboro to Raleigh-Durham, North Carolina, and I went on to San Francisco, California. In San Francisco, the flight swelled as we were joined by more military personnel; army, marines, and airmen.

After having been greeted by little children at the airport in San Francisco, we flew to Hickam Air Force Base, Hawaii. From Hawaii, we flew across the International Date Line, way up over Australia. We would take on fuel on Wake Island, a small Island, managed by the US Air Force, about three quarters of the way across the Pacific Ocean. We had to stay over a couple of days in the Philippine Islands, the home of Clark Air Force base, where we did M-16 training.

Now we were on our last leg of our trip to South Vietnam. I think we went off course, or we may have gotten high jacked or something. Because I don't think we made Tan Son Nhut. We landed somewhere in Vietnam. Could it have been Hanoi in the communist North? Since Hanoi was only about ten miles north of Ton San hut?Don't Know. But there is one thing for certain; the sweet, loud noise of those four engines was silenced almost immediately after touchdown. The airplane sat on a narrow taxi way. We were allowed to deplane and stretched our legs for a brief period. Then we were asked to get back on the plane.

Even though that Charlie 130 was suddenly silenced, she welcomed us back inside, and she protected us from possible harm, like a hen protects her chicks. We sat there a long time. Then a midsized yellow tug came and hooked on to her and towed her toward a hanger. She held on tight to us as she limped along behind the tug. I don't remember much else, but I do recall though, that a few Air Force personnel and I ended up at Don Muang Air Base in Thailand, near Bangkok. The army and marine personnel stayed behind. I've been trying for fifty-one years or more to recall the specifics of what happened, but it isn't here. So then, I guess they didn't tell me much.

At Don Muang, we did a minimum of in processing the first day because the host was more concerned about getting us to a place to refresh and rest. This was perceived to have been a simple process, and it was, I guess. Except that my expectations were that I would be living in a dormitory environment on base. When in reality, dormitory space was limited to E-3s and below, and E-4s and above were required to live on the economy.

This was troubling to me because I was not financially prepared to do this. I had just recently been promoted to E-4 and I had a family back home. It was a pain. But what would life be without the pain? I'll get through it, I thought. Because of my ordination, the wisdom of good fortune was with me. The non-commissioned officers with whom I was traveling, felt my pain and they took me under their wings.

They took me under their wing, especially Technical Sergeant Lusk, a gray-headed gentleman who was getting on toward retirement age. TSgt Lusk rallied the other troops to make sure that I had the basic needs of food, shelter, and to get me settled in. So I got through it.

I was so much appreciative, and I paid all of my debts in time. Now, with my basic needs of food and shelter met, all that I needed was my luggage, especially my fatigues so I could get to work. My luggage would not catch up with me for nine days or so. Therefore, I wore my 1505s, a beige and cotton semi-dress uniform as a work uniform. The uniform was safe to wear around aircraft and petroleum products, but it had to be washed and pressed every night. Other than having just the three stripes on my sleeves, the uniform gave the impression that I was someone in authority around the aircraft.

Not so. Our mission was to provide jet fuel support to a sub squadron of F-102 fighter interceptors. We were also responsible for jet fuel and demineralized water for the KC-135 tankers that did air to air refueling to extend fighter flights over Vietnam and elsewhere in the region. Everything was going well with our mission. It's kind of funny how people take notice of the smallest sign of initiative.

Some people in positions of authority thought I showed extraordinary initiative to not wait around for my utility uniforms to arrive; the way that I made do with my cotton semi dress uniform for work, but I didn't know any better. I just knew that they needed me. So I pitched in and helped. Many days, I would stay on the flight line all day. I would take short lunch breaks. I didn't think that anything would come of it because I was used to working anyway. But after I had been in country about two months, my unit started screening people to go on temporary duty (TDY) to the aerospace fuels laboratory school in Tachikawa (Tachi), Japan. Those two people would be required to learn how to set up, manage, and operate a regional aerospace fuels laboratory.

The purpose of this lab and its people was to cross check or correlate fuel samples from all across the region, and make sure that our jets and reciprocating engine aircraft were being serviced with the highest quality of petroleum products. My unit needed a Technical Sergeant (TSgt) E6 supervisor, and an Airman first class E4 technician for this very important assignment. They choose TSgt William Baker as supervisor, and they chose me as technician. I was surprised.

I was surprised, because by my own will, I had put other airmen ahead of myself. It's a feeling you get. Some days, somehow, you just get that feeling of uncertainty, you know? And I was, quite frankly, hoping that they would pick someone else. But I knew that it was not good to complain, and I didn't, even though I did have some issues. I was thinking about the South China Sea and the Tan Son Nhut experience that I had coming over. I was concerned about overstressing my budget. I would lose contact with my wife and loved ones back home for a while. I would have to awaken my knowledge of the science of chemistry to be able to do the required chemistry procedures effectively to work in a fuels laboratory. These were real issues for me, but I pressed through anyway. How could I not press through?

My sister Betty, a great testimonial evangelist and mother of 8 children.

I believe my parents and siblings, being an interceding family, were praying for my increased faith. Because when I lost my anxiety, I said another prayer. Then, I said, I'd better run on. I'd better run on and see how my faith will grow. We headed out over the South China Sea, an arm of the Pacific Ocean. We were flying from Don Muang Air Base, near Bangkok, Thailand to Tan Son Nhut Air Base, near Saigon, South Vietnam. Our final destination was Tachikawa (Tachi), Japan.

Sister Levon (Bonnie) C. Ward and her husband, the late Cecil Ward, Bonnie is a Holy Spirit led intercessor and mother of 4 children.

17

Engine Picked Over Tan Son Nhut, Bridge Over Troubled Water

We got through a terrifyingly rough landing at Tan Son Nhut. There was overhead luggage on top of people who were thrown into the isle. It was no one's fault. It was just that we had to land in a hurry after having been kept on final approach for an extended period of time. After we landed and taxied to our parking spot, the reception area was adorned with greeters. The greeters at Tan Son Nhut were superbly impressive in appearance. They were all young women dressed in beautiful turquoise and white appropriately fitted uniforms. They all looked noble, and of hand-picked appointment. This single observance made it that much clearer that we may have gotten off course, and we were possibly highjacked on our way over the first time.

Remember that flight where we lost an engine and then almost lost our second one? The Lord must have heard my mother's prayer, because we averted the Philippine Islands and we took a course toward communist South China; perhaps that was the way of the wind. The number two engine regained enough strength to help us to maintain a low, but steady altitude. Surely, the Lord built a bridge over troubled water for us that day. Now, maintaining a low, but steady altitude, we hobbled our way on over to Hung Shun air base on the Island of Formosa, in communist South China. Many thanks to God for our safe arrival on dry land again. At Hung Shun, we got some mechanical help for the number two engine. The aircraft was refueled, to include taking on an anti-detonation inhibitor

(ADI). ADI is a liquid cooling agent that gives reciprocating engines more thrust when injected into the engine on takeoff. The passengers were allowed to leave the aircraft and refresh themselves while these operations were taking place. I was glad to be leaving the airplane because I urgently needed to refresh my bladder.

The crewmembers detained me and made me a courier for the remainder of the flight. "A courier is a messenger, esp. one on official diplomatic business. Or a personal attendant hired to make arrangements for a journey." The crewmembers fitted me with a belt and a holster. Then they put a long pistol in the holster, and I was given strict instructions not to let anything happen to that airplane.

I have no idea why they choose me to be courier. Except, sometimes, God just wants to get you alone to administer to you. But I suspect that it was because I was the lowest ranking military person on the airplane at E-4. I suspect, also, that the reason they choose me as courier is because they probably knew that I would not in any way abuse or misuse the weapon. The ADI truck operator was admiring the large weapon on my side just before he started the ADI replenishing operation. About half way through the operation, the ADI truck caught fire. The fire frightened the operator so badly that he started running away. And I started yelling to him, stop, stop, come back!

Come back! I screamed repeatedly, but he kept running. Then I thought that I should use the word halt because surely, the word halt must be of the universal language. So I then yelled halt as loudly as I could yell. He halted and he immediately came back. By quick action and total determination, we were able to get the vehicle unhooked from the aircraft and moved to a safe distance away from the aircraft. There was little damage to the truck, and there was no ^damage to the aircraft, thank god. We saved the airplane, and soon, the maintenance crew would be finished.

When the maintenance crew finished, I was free to go and empty my aching bladder. The passengers re-boarded the airplane, and we made another run for the Philippines and Clark Air Force Base. I traveled alone in a small space in the back of the airplane to the Philippines. I had only my gun and a silver sack about the size of a hospital laundry bag to watch. There was something inside of the bag. I was forbidden to know what it was, but I had strict orders not to let nobody touch that sack. Therefore,

I was truly alone with my God; a gun and the silver sack all the way from Formosa to the Philippines. We stayed at Clark a few days; and eventually, we flew on to Tachikawa, Japan. TSgt Baker and I successfully completed the aerospace fuels laboratory school, which we originally set out to do.

18

Character Investigation and Working with Air Force One

We returned to the long hours of work. A handful of us flight line troops had to stay late to service some transient F-105 fighter jets. The transient aircraft unexpectedly dropped in on us. It was December 1965. There was a show taking place on base. It was the Bob Hope Christmas show. Even though we were a little late arriving at the show, and all the regular seats were taken, we were lucky.

We were lucky because we were given seats on the back of a flatbed truck that was close to the stage. The flatbed was used as a structure for the entertainers waiting area. We could see everything!

The show featured, Carol Baker, Joey Heatherton, the Nicolas brothers, Anita Bryant and Jack Jones. Also, there were, Kaye Stevens, Dianna Lynn Bates, and Jerry Colonna. This was truly a magnificent Bob Hope show. Also, I saw the world famous vibes player and bandleader, Lionel Hampton, who came to Bangkok during my tour. This was gratifying entertainment for those serving so far, far away from home. Not withstanding the unrelentingly hot, Southeast Asian sun, and the long working hours; my tour in Southeast Asia was fairly routine, until the personnel section started doing background checks on certain people. I was one of them. I didn't have a clue of what the background checks were about, but I did get some strange invites to dine with people that I would not normally be personally associated with. They were in upper management. But later, I learned that the Air Force was streamlining personnel to work with Air Force One. I was, therefore, the subject of a parallel investigation for character flaws, character history for both overseas, and in my hometown back in Cartersville, Georgia. As a result of the investigation, I was cleared and handpicked for my next assignment. My next assignment was Andrews Air Force Base, Maryland, home of Air Force One.

At Andrews, I was assigned to the Fuels Management Branch as one of the refueling Supervisors for Air Force One and the Presidential Aircraft Fleet, a very humbling position. Air Force One, at the time, was a VC-137C, with Air Force serial number 62-6000. Special Air Missions (SAM) 26000 was a customized Boeing 707. President Kennedy first flew on the aircraft on November 10, 1962, to attend the funeral services of former First Lady Eleanor Roosevelt in Hyde Park, New York.

We at fuels were also required to enthusiastically work with other aircraft as well. But Air Force One 26000 was special to work with because she was, and still is, even though retired, the most famous and the most prestigious. It was once was the most highly secured airplane in the universe. She was *America's airplane*.

She transported the most powerful person in the universe, the President of the United States, and other very powerful people. Prior presidential aircraft were designated as Eagle One. My having worked with the very first Air Force One in history, attests to my mother's words in chapter eleven, "if you stay close to the umbilical card that fed you, you will go places, and do things that are uncommon to lowly people."

19
Other Experiences at Andrews AFB-Home of Air Force One

My family and I arrived at Andrews Air Force Base, Maryland in July 1966. This was truly a measure of good fortune. My good fortune continued to follow me for a while, and then it turned sour for a while. It was because of a promotion. I was promoted to staff sergeant E-5 out of cycle. The promotion came in August 1966 between the June 1966 and October 1966 promotion cycles. No one in my chain of command had ever heard of anyone getting promoted out of cycle. Neither had I. There were people who thought it was unfair that my promotion came with just five years and one month total service. The promotion caused a stir because rank was hard to make back then. Some people told me that they had troops with twelve, fifteen, and eighteen years or more total service, and they were still looking for E5. So with that on their minds, I ran into a stumbling block. I stumbled when I missed base detail. The missed detail was Non-Commissioned Officer of the Day (NCOD). The bulletin board was posted while I was on a two-day break and away from the base. There would be administrative action for missing an appointment.

When I went before my first sergeant and my administrative officer, they warned me up front that the punishment was pretty harsh. Saying, "you're young and you can get over this. We have to send a message to some of our older, personnel who aren't performing as well as they can."

Then the ole man, my commander, dropped the hammer. The harsh punishment read in part as follows:

- Article-15, which in your case species the following:
- Reduction in rank, from E-5 to E-4,
- Forfeiture of one third of your base pay per month for three months.
- The performance of twenty-one consecutive days of extra duty @ two hours a day.
- The forfeiture of the position of Mister Vice for the upcoming dinning in.

And more.

Here, I must say, though, the ole man gave me a big, and much appreciated break. The reduction in rank and the forfeiture of pay were suspended.

Article 15s, as crippling as they have the potential of being, had its targeted effect. I vowed not to duplicate a mistake from that day on. Things happen. I looked at the article as a good athlete might. Sometimes, a good athlete has to take one for the team. I, being an athlete, I believe I served that purpose. I took one for the team. But nevertheless, I was promoted to E-6 in the minimum time in less than two years.

When I looked around, I realized that I never had anything like this to happen to me. But when I looked back, I realized that I just blew it that time. Yet, I had my conscious and my doctrine of home training of doing what's good and what's right, and doing my best. I hoped that my best was good enough. I believe, if you are doing these things, favor will hunt you down and bless you. I felt blessed to have my highly scrutinized and totally mission-essential job working with so many airplanes. Working with the very best in the universe, Air Force One 26000, and her ground crew, made me fight to do my very, very, best always. This had a bright, positive, and lasting effect on me.

20
Educational Experiences at Andrews

Even though the working environment was great and filled with light, there were some situations surrounding off base living conditions that were filled with darkness. The first apartment that we rented was near St. Elizabeth mental institution. We lived at Alabama Place, South East, in Washington D.C. My sponsor and others highly recommended that I rent an apartment in that area, but there were issues with the apartment.

The first issue was a tree had grown up by one of the bedroom windows. The second issue was parking was on the backside of the apartment. The third issue was you had to walk through an enclosed passageway with your belongings in order to get to the front side of the building- to gain entrance to your apartment. The fourth issue was that mostly every afternoon, there would be men, and sometimes a woman or two sitting with their feet and legs obstructing the enclosed area and drinking. The fifth issue was that sometimes, there would be unsightly debris near the enclosed passageway; these issues and more made living in the apartment very unpleasant. There were catcalls, and my wife was terrified of the catcalls. The aggressive behavior of some of the men was very inappropriate, and this was our new home.

My wife and I went to the landlord several times seeking to get our security deposit back. We wanted to move, but we were locked into an agreement for the apartment for one year, if we were to have our security deposit returned, we would stay a little longer. The longer we stayed, the worse things got. Then, a possible life-threatening issue came up, and we had to move security deposit or not.

One sunny day around noon, while I was at work, a group of men gathered at the tree, the one that had grown up by one of the bedroom windows. The would-be intruders were encouraging one another to climb the tree and enter our apartment while my wife and child were inside. My wife hid the child; and all that she had for self-defense was her prayers, her faith, and a claw hammer in her right hand. Since we had not gotten telephone service installed, and there were no cell phones back then, I was not notified of the incident until I arrived back home later that afternoon. Not having a phone only added to her fright. The men, realizing how frightening they were, finally came to themselves. They left without incident.

The place was frightening at high twelve; even on the brightest, sun shiny days, the place was frightening. And at low twelve, you tried not to entertain the darkness; for it had its own miseries. We saw more misery and pain while we were living in that place, than ever we saw rejoicing. There was rejoicing though, however, as I called around, inquiring about other apartments to rent. I would inquire about apartments in D.C. as well as in Maryland. Some of the apartment managers in Maryland were very positive when I would talk to them on the phone. I would ask them if they had a vacancy, and their reply would be in the positive. Sometimes, they would encourage me, by saying that children would love the vacant apartment; the apartment is on the ground floor, and it is right across from the playground. But when I would show up to view the apartment, the apartment that had been confirmed to be vacant just an hour ago, would have just been rented; obviously, they were not renting to people of color.

This unfortunate situation helped my wife and me to settle on another apartment. This time, we moved to an apartment complex on Southern Avenue in Washington D.C. We lived there comfortably for a while. But you could see the quality of life in those apartments begin to slip away, as the garbage bins began to constantly overflow due to inadequate service. This apartment complex was a good place to live, even though some of the services were slipping away and it was a long way from my work. We stayed because discriminatory practices were a problem in off base housing for service men of color in that area.

But when the Secretary of Defense, Mr. Robert S. McNamara turned his attention to the problem of discrimination in off base housing for service men of color in 1967; the Secretary quickly decided to use sanctions against a discriminatory practice widely accepted and still legal under Federal Law at the time.

Mr. McNamara's memo for Secretaries of military departments, 22 June 67 Subject: Unsatisfactory Housing of Negro Military Families Living off-post in the Andrews Air Force Base Area, S D Files.

Shortly after this decree, my family and I moved into an apartment complex just across from Andrews, air force base, in Camp springs, Maryland.

Please don't miss understand me, there were available, nice, luxurious apartments in D.C. However, they were economically out of reach for a lot of military service personnel. Therefore, from an economical point of view, the move had its personal rewards. The savings on vehicle operations by living close to the base vs. the expenditures on vehicle operations while living in D.C. were immediately noticeable.

It was easier and much less expensive to get too my job. With the move, we could more richly discharge our civic duties and participate in community affairs. We attended church services on the base. My wife and I were better able to supplement my military income by working on the base. I worked a part time job, and my wife worked fulltime, much of the time. In addition to working extra, we were able to avidly support the American Youth Association (AYA). Our work with the AYA primarily focused on little league baseball. My wife was team mother for our sons' team, and she was an excellent leader for children. I coached, and our sons and teammates played and learned the beautiful game of base ball.

The peace of mind from living in a well maintained apartment and a safe environment helped improve the military readiness posture from my point of view. And I am reasonability assured that many black GI's shared this view. We owe many thanks to the Secretary of Defense, Mr. Robert S. McNamara.

21
Fall Out from Dr. Martin Luther King's Assassination

On April 4, 1968, we had a very real and unforgettable visit to Washington. The visit was about a breaking news story. The newscasters were busy telling the world about the renowned civil rights leader, Dr. Martin Luther King's assignation in Memphis, Tennessee. My wife and I were curious, as were many others. There was much concern for Dr. King, and there was concern for the city because of possible burning and looting. So after work that day, we drove from Camp Springs to 14th street in Washington D.C.

We had planned to turn around immediately if we saw any sign of violence or looting. Unfortunately, though, there were so many curious people that we got stuck. We were hindered from turning around because the authorities were blocking off the streets adjacent to fourteenth. As we slowly moved along, we saw firsthand looting and burning of businesses. We saw business owners painting "soul brother" on their businesses.

They were trying to sway the looters not to take from them or burn their establishments. Yet, there were people carrying console model TVs, smaller TVs, and other merchandise. The people, who appeared to have been looting, were just walking down the sidewalk beside our cars with their stuff. Some of the people appeared to have been in a hurry, but they didn't appear to be in the least frightened. But in reality, the situation in which we found ourselves was indeed frightening. In fact, it was so scary that my wife, Barbara, took cover on the floor in the back of the car with our children for more assured safety.

And with the grace of my maker, I was able to lead my family to safety on the other side of the city in time. In the days ahead, certain parts of Washington, D.C. became a fiery inferno. The fiery inferno ignited over the assassination of Dr. Martin Luther King. King was telling the world that he was ready to face his maker. He had lead so brilliantly while under relentless stress, and he had helped so many people in his lifetime. An excerpt from his I've Been to the Mountaintop speech in some ways speaks to this. Also, in some ways, Dr. King's I've Been to the Mountaintop's speech parallels the Great Prophet Moses mountain top experience as depicted in Deuteronomy 34:1–5.

The following is an excerpt from Dr. King's, I've Been to the Mountaintop speech:

> Well, I don't know what will happen now. We've got some difficult days ahead. But it really doesn't matter with me now, because I've been to the mountaintop. And I don't mind. Like anybody, I'd like to live a long life. Longevity has its place. But I'm not concerned about that now. I just want to do God's will. And he's allowed me to go up to the mountain. And I've looked over. And I've seen the promised- land. I may not get there with you. But I want you to know tonight, that we, as a people, will get to the promised land! And so I'm happy tonight. I'm not worried about anything. I'm not fearing any man. Mine eyes have seen the glory of the coming of the Lord!! And Dr. King died there in Memphis, that night.

Moses' mountaintop experience–Deuteronomy 34:1–5:

> Then Moses climbed Mount Nebo from the plains of Moab to the top of Pisgah, across from Jericho. There the Lord showed him the whole land- from Gilead to Dan, all of Naphtali, the territory of Ephraim and Manasseh, all the land of Judah as far as the western sea, the Negev and the whole region from the valley of Jericho, the city of Palms, as far as Zoar. Then the Lord said to him, "This is the land I promised on oath to Abraham, Isaac and Jacob when I said, 'I will give it to your descendants.' I have let you see it with your eyes, but you will not cross over into it."

And Moses the servant of the lord died there in Moab, as the Lord had said. As sure as death came to the great Dr. Martin Luther, King and the great prophet Moses, it's a surety that the same fate will come to us all. As time passed while I was at Andrews, I lost family members, friends, many fellow comrades in the Vietnam War, and others I may not have personally known, but admired nonetheless.

Even though President John Fitzgerald Kennedy was assassinated on November 22, 1963, his presence was always felt when I approached his airplane, Air Force One. I had grown too close to it all. But by the steady hand of God, I got through the losses and I moved on, but I was torn.

As torn as I was about moving on from Andrews Air Force Base, I looked back. And in looking back, I realized how diligently God had provided for me there. And something in my "spirit" said, "go on from here. Go on, increase your territory, and widen your borders." And by the end of July 1970, I departed Andrews Air Force Base for Wiesbaden, Germany. I departed Andrews with a good name. And I also departed with a little league baseball championship on the line. But the coaches, my wife, and the players assured me that they would win the championship for me, and they won!

22

Assigned to Wiesbaden AB Germany

My name preceded me to Germany. I had already won there as well. Those in my duty section thought it was extra ordinary that someone had come to them from an assignment working with Air Force One. But our mission in Wiesbaden was quite different. We were dedicated to servicing KC-97 inflight refueling aircraft, a handful of C130s used for seeding the clouds to make the heavy fog go away so that other aircraft could take off and land safely when the fog was extremely heavy. We also serviced a few cargo and VIP aircraft.

I was in middle management and in charge of most of the young troops. The young troops thought that I could solve any problem, whether job related or personal. I learned much about them while I learned the technical and procedural side of my job. And at the same time, I was coordinating the arrival of my family.

My family joined me in September 1970 after I found shelter for them. My family and I were very excited to be together again, and we were excited to be in Germany. My wife was in such a rush to join me that I had no time to compare apartments. Our first two years in Germany, we lived in downtown Wiesbaden in an apartment inside a closed court on Saalgasse Strasse. Then we moved into the Hainerburg housing area, one of the military off base housing complexes. Our sons attended American schools, both elementary and high school. After getting everything coordinated, everything went extremely smoothly. With everything going extremely well, on the job and at home, I was able to participate in some personal initiatives on my- off duty time.

Some of the initiatives that I participated in were:

- Working part time as Night Manager at the Non-Commissioned Officer's Club
- Coaching little league base ball
- Taking college courses
- Playing National Collegiate Athletic Association (NCAA) level or perhaps, semi-pro level football. I played in the Continental Sports Conference (CSC) with the awesome Wiesbaden Flyers in 1972 and 1973. The CSC was an excellent morale booster, and source of entertainment for military personnel, and their families who were away from home. Players who were talented enough almost felt it a sense of duty to participate in CSC activities.
- I received my third degree in free masonry; and I completed studies in free masonry through the thirty-second degree. However, the fourth degree through the thirty-second degree was not conferred on me due to a prior commitment to little league baseball during the weekend of conference. It was my conscious to help youngsters grow, and help them become responsible, and productive citizens through dedicated teamwork and good sportsmanship associated with playing little league baseball.

As you can see, with my military duties, and my off duty extracurricular activities, I kept a very busy schedule. However, during the consecutive five-year period we were stationed in Germany, we combined off duty time and vacation time. Therefore, my, family and I were able to travel together, learn the culture and visit some of the many interesting sites.

In our travels, we cruised on the famed Rhine River; traveled to Holland, Denmark, Austria and my wife accompanied the boys to Spain for a little League baseball tournament. Learning the culture was fairly easy. After being in a certain environment for a given period, you just adapt to your surroundings. In our case, we learned the German language to a comfortable degree; we commingled with the people; and we just naturally learned to enjoy the Octoberfest, soccer, and parades. Jaeger schnitzel, Weiner schnitzel, Bratwurst, and a bit of cold German beer were also enjoyable. Visiting various sites was interesting as well as educational.

Among the sites we visited were, Hitler's Eagles nest at Berchtesgaden, Germany. "The lodge which sits like a James Bond fantasy atop an alpine peak-was a gift to Adolph Hitler. The gift was for Adolph's fiftieth birthday in 1939. His inner circle all contributed." (picture)

We visited the salt mines at Berchtesgaden. The salt mines features an underground lake. We visited the 1972 summer Olympics stadium in Munich, Germany. We also visited Neuschwanstein castle, the black forest, a storied furniture-manufacturing region, and other interesting sites. Serving my country while traveling, and learning a new culture was an unforgettable experience. And it was the highlight of my family's life. By July 1975, I had certainly increased my territory and widened my borders, as it must have been in my fate to do. Now, it was time to move on, and it was still yet Before Dawn.

23
Assigned to Pease AFB, New Hampshire

I knew beforehand that I had been assigned to the Strategic Air Command (SAC) on my return to the United States. It was only a matter of which state side base I'd be assigned to. At first, I was to be assigned to Kincheloe Air Force Base near Sault Ste. Marie, Michigan and Ontario, Canada. Then it was March Air Force Base, Riverside County, California. March Air Force Base would have been an ideal place to be stationed with the warm weather and all. However, SAC needed to fill an immediate opening for a Master Sergeant in my career field at Pease. Since I had recently been promoted to Master Sergeant and was in transit, they rerouted me up to Pease Air Force Base, Portsmouth, New Hampshire to fill the position.

My wife, Barbara, and I left behind our many friends, both military and German. Our faithful friends, staff sergeant Howard and Mrs. Bernadera Franklin, and their baby Lisa, kept our sons Reggie and Carl for three weeks. The boys stayed behind to travel with the European little league baseball all-star team to Gary, Indiana; where they played in the 1975 little League World Series. The Franklins weren't just friends that pass by only once. They were friends from the heart. You know, godly friends, who were always there for you, the kinds you can trust. We are forever grateful for their kindness and grace.

My report date didn't correlate with the tournament dates. Therefore, Barb and I went on ahead to Pease. We had stopped for a brief visit in New Haven, Connecticut with Barbara's relatives. After the World Series, our sons were stranded for a very watchful night at LaGuardia Airport in New

York City. However, we were able to reunite with them after they traveled by limousine to relatives in New Haven.

The Cooleys, Reggie top left, Carl top right, Barbara bottom left, Ralph Riley bottom right.

Now, with the family intact, I continued working to see how I could help the SAC mission to flourish. I was assigned to the 509th Bombardment Wing as Fuels Operations Superintendent. Apparently, there had been some issues that needed attention such as morale, on time refueling support, and quasi performance on Operational Readiness Inspections (ORI). We were locked up in service to the tanker cargo KC-135, inflight-refueling squadron, who yet had a commitment to the cold war. The 509th was also committed to flying the super swift and mighty powerful fighter-bombers FB-111 Aardvark. The fighter-bombers were all weather flying machines that carried nuclear weapons. World peace leaned heavily on the performance of the FB-111s at Pease and other aircraft around the globe. We at fuels knew that we could not turn one wheel on the assigned aircraft without safe, efficient, timely, alert fuel service, and service with the highest quality of jet fuel. Our commanders knew it, the Iranians knew it, and the Russians knew it. There were senior staff and middle managers in place at my post. However, my commander looked to me to lead and to get the job done. We had to get it done.

To get it done, militarily, some might argue that this was the perfect time to be harsh and condemning. But when you're working with young people, many of whom who felt that they were unfairly treated, millions, and millions of gallons of volatile jet fuel, high powered jet air craft, and nuclear weapons. I was not comfortable with the philosophy of harsh and condemning treatment. I, instead, choose to be tender and strong. The first thing we needed to do was to learn to respect each other.

Our people needed to learn to treat each other with dignity and that we were all there to carry out the mission of the United States air force, safely, and in a most excellent way. We taught and stressed the importance of the mission; we taught how good attitudes of each individual, and how each individual doing excellent work would strengthen us. We trained to that end, and then there was the representation factor. We assured all of our people that they would be appropriately represented to the commander, and the commander to them; and that their records would be documented, and made competitive air force wide. With all of this said and done, you could see the pride in the organization come alive. Morale and job performance soared. Our people were committed to dependability, trust worthiness, hard work excellence, and unwavering dedication to duty.

We all were committed to excellence. I was committed to excellence in character, excellence to our people, excellence to my commanders, the mission, and excellence in leadership. My commander put the responsibility of the Fuels Management branch squarely upon my shoulders. I had to lead, or get out of the way. As a result of all of all our efforts, we helped the 509th bombardment Wing get all of its fighter-bombers operationally ready (OR) and cocked on safely, and on time. As a result, we received an excellent rating on the 1977 Strategic Air Command Inspector General Inspection.

Despite all the hard work, I found the time and energy to coach the squadron's men's softball team. We won the base championship. This helped the 509th Supply squadron to win the coveted commanders trophy for 1977. The entire base effort was about doing our jobs superbly, and winning. Winners are awarded.

Through the commanders' extensive awards system, many people were recognized. For me, I was just glad to have had favor with God who wisely guarded me in my strength, and that I was able to help out. However, the Strategic Air Command (SAC) recognized me as the Fuels Superintendent of the year, and first runner up for best in the Air force. My records were superbly documented, and made tops for special assignments and promotions. Being from the South, I was published in Who's, who in the South, that year.

Although from the South, I had not had much contact with my people in the South over the past sixteen years. Except on bereavement occasions, or on short visits when transferring to the next station. Otherwise, I couldn't see my people. But Levon (Bonnie), my baby sister changed that when she and her husband, Cecil Ward, drove from Cartersville, Georgia to Portsmouth, NH with their children, Andre, Monica, Cedric, and Brett to visit my family and me in 1977. It was a blessed and welcomed visit. The weather was chilly in the mornings and afternoons while they were here.

But it wasn't anything like what we experienced during the devastating blizzard that struck on February 6, 1978. One of the worst winter storms that ever landed on New England. The storm left so much snow and ice that the fighter-bombers had to be parked in plowed out parallel rows. And the grounding rings could only be found by the use of metal detectors. The storm was harsher to some than others, but we got through it. Then, my mother and my aunt, Beatrice (Aunt B), flew up and visited us in the summer of 1978.

This was my mother's first time flying, I believe. She came to attend my son, Reggie's, high school graduation.

24

The Middle East-Kunsan AB Korea Taking the Fight North

At the time, I was on orders to go to Tehran, Iran as an adviser to the Iranian Air Force. Perhaps, everyone went there as an adviser. This assignment was supposed to be tight-lipped. I especially wanted it kept secret from my dear mother. Because she was somewhat familiar with the Middle Eastern culture, she would worry; but the assignment was no secret to her.

I believe my mother was a seer, or a prophetess, because this resourceful matriarch could discern things. "You, as a military entity will fulfill the assignment, and serve honorably, if indeed, it is a just and up right assignment, but if it is not just," she said, "you will be spared the journey." In as much as I wanted to go, I was spared. Due to political issues between President Carter and the Shah of Iran, the President put a freeze on sending more Americans to Iran. And my assignment was cancelled later in 1978. The political issue between our President and the Shah led to the 444-day siege usually referred to as the hostage crisis. It was only by fate that I did not become a hostage. I stayed on at Pease, the remainder of 1978. But I was overdue for a second remote assignment.

Since I was overdue for a second remote assignment, I found myself at Kunsan air base, South Korea by the end of January 1979, a true remote. South Korea's closest neighbors are communist North Korea, Japan, and, China. Kunsan air base is located on the Western side of the South Korean

Peninsula, bordered by the yellow sea. The attitude of the base was like a big happy family, everyone was helping and encouraging everyone else.

Kunsan also was a hard-working base, and as a friendly gesture, everywhere you went on the base you could hear, "no slack on the kun." It was all about the fight, and the 8th (TFW) Tactical Fighter Wing's ability to take the fight North. The 8th TFW was flying the muscle bound, strong, twin-engine F-4 phantom fighter jets in 1979. The F-4 pilots were eager, determined, and very highly skilled. Therefore, the 8th could, without question, take the fight North, and to wherever, and deliver its lethal air power whenever directed by the proper authority. The F-4s were true to their mission as long as they got the proper ground support. The young troops provided outstanding support capabilities as expected, but the F-4 was getting old. It was especially comforting, and re-enforcing of confidence to see the well-seasoned master sergeants, senior masters, and chiefs advising, and figuring out tough situations for the young-insuring mission integrity, and continuity. It was like being in the presence of military Geniuses.

These men earned that respect by years of study, and years of working hard at their craft. My career took an upward turn by way of promotion to senior master sergeant (E-8) while I was at Kunsan. My promotion caught everyone by surprise, and it didn't go over very well. I think, for one reason, my promotion didn't go over very well was because I presented very young for my age and responsibilities. Thus, I was tagged with the nickname, "teen age master sergeant." Another reason I think my promotion didn't go over too well was that other people were consumed with getting promoted to E-8, and they were not promoted. But what they didn't know was that I tested well that cycle, thank god. I had thirteen consecutive years of perfect well- appointed records. And the Strategic Air Command (SAC) recognized me as a one hundred percenter, and that sealed the promotion.

For some reason, promotions came easy for me; but promotions always plagued me. Even though my promotion to E-8 was a blessing, the promotion set me up to be a sacrifice. A sacrifice, you say? Well, it all started one Friday, late in the afternoon, at about the normal shift change time. The Commander In Chief Pacific Air Command (CINCPAC), with his Operational Readiness Inspection Team (ORI) dropped in on Kunsan, un-announced. My job that night was flight line coordinator/supervisor for fuels. We went immediately into an aircraft generation mode, whereby innocent fighter aircraft were reconfigured, made war ready with warheads, and reconfigured fuel loads. And strict aircraft maintenance is key. Another key was the recall of personnel.

The recall went well, the majority of the troops were on base any way. As a matter of fact, the whole generation was going well; we were ahead of schedule until around midnight. But at midnight, a driving, sustained rain came upon us, and caused a delay. I had never seen it rain so hard, anywhere, ever. We were able, however, to get every aircraft done, maintenance, munitions, and fuel-all ahead of time, except one air craft.

Our young fuels people were outstanding under hectic conditions. They were on those fighter jets like ordained peace speakers. They worked in close harmony with the aircraft maintenance crews, the weapons crews, and their weapons jammers. However, the last aircraft was parked on the lowest parking spot on the parking ramp. All the spare aircraft were taken earlier. So we had no choice but to work that airplane. We had to wait for the water to drain so that the weapons jammer vehicles could get in.

When fuels tried to perform its operation, the aircraft would not take on fuel. It apparently caught a vapor lock, according to the experts, due to the heavy down pour, and having stood in an uncommon amount of water for an extended period of time. We tried everything to get the F-4s fuel system to feed. We pressurized and depressurized the system again, and again. We changed fueling units, and insured all valves were open. The aircraft's fueling system was recycled several times. We concluded that this was not a manmade problem; if it were, we had the people there who could fix it. Crew chiefs from other aircraft were there encouraging and shouting instruction from outside the safety zone. Many of the military geniusess were there, including an officer who was a major. This aircraft put us through a typical hurry up and wait ordeal, if you ever saw one. We would hurry up and get things done, and then, wait to see what the aircraft was going to do. Sometimes, you just have to wait. Only this time, peoples' careers were just waiting to be destroyed, but we were not going down just yet.

And while we still had time to declare the aircraft operationally ready (OR), somehow, the command post was falsely informed that the aircraft would fall short of mission ready status at the proper time. It was around five o'clock in the morning. We were at "A Hour," plus. I was praying. We all were praying, but they won't tell you that. You can't manage such complex machines, as those bomber and fighter jets, less the hand of God is on you. And lucky for the team, the aircraft dropped his vapor lock, and we brought him up to the war fuel load just under the wire.

All of the flight line troops and supervisors were elated that we had successfully passed the generation phase of the mini ORI. We all went happily on our separate ways to debriefings. At our debriefing, I found my supervisors edgy and wrathful, which was unusual for them. But if you were not actually on the flight line, the word was out that we had failed. Despite all the adverse issues that developed during the exercise, the intense rain, the delay brought on by natural causes, the aircraft's fuel system vapor lock, I owned the responsibility for fuels operations. So, breathe in humbly, if there was blame to be, the blame was on me. As sure as our flying mission was to take the fight north; there were consequences.

As a result, of a short conversation with my officer in charge, I was abruptly fired. After receiving such a greeting, I was weak and broken. Because we poured out our hearts for the mission, trying to make sure that we didn't go down in defeat. But as I thought about it, and when you look at it head on, it wasn't good enough. We were flirting with peace, international security, and potentially peoples' freedom and lives. "You've got to get fuel into those jets, all of them." I mocked myself. "If you can't get fuel into them, they won't fly." You see, it's like being stuck in your garage in your car with your very ill child. If you can't get the car to go, you're helpless. But this was about taking the fight North. We looked helpless, I suppose, to our guest who were there to ascertain if we could, in fact take the fight North.

25

The Yellow Sea and Maxwell AFB, Alabama

I was tired, weak, and broken. I knew that I needed some time alone to regain my strength. So when I departed the office, instead of going up to the barracks to my room, I turned right on to the perimeter road and headed down toward the yellow sea. I worried as I lumbered along. If you have ever seen a poor soul who worries too much, you know that excessive worrying is bad for his/her mental state.

So to protect my mental health, I redirected my attitude from worrying to just being concerned. My deep concern for the outcome of my job performance was somewhat relieved by the gentleness of the yellow sea. I was always intrigued with the yellow sea. One reason, I guess, is it isn't very deep. It is only about a half mile in depth. The yellow sea, is called the yellow sea, because of the sand particles from the Gobi Desert sand storms that turn the surface of the water into a golden yellow. Silt from the yellow and Hai He River contribute to the sea color.

It was a long slow walk down to the yellow sea. As I walked, I talked to my heavenly Father; and I am not ashamed to say it, I talked to him about bringing closure to the wrath that I met with earlier. In my heart, I knew that if everything had gone smoothly during the exercise, there would not have been any wrath. Wrath, I had no control over that, but I knew God was in control. I asked for mercy, "O Lord, in wrath, remember, mercy, as stated in Habakkuk 3: 2. As I continued my slow walk toward the sea, I was haunted by possibly causing unfavorable inspection results. But God would surely be merciful. Then, reality set in. Did I really get fired, or am I being sacrificed? Would I mind being sacrificed? Absolutely not, if it was for the greater good, like saving someone else's career. After all, it was about taking the fight North. We could take it to the North Koreans, absolutely. The 8th, the wolf pack, could take the fight North any time, or anywhere as deemed necessary by the proper authority-and with success. By observing the devotion to duty and the will of all assigned personnel, sealed my confidence. Furthermore, confidence was up on the water of the yellow sea.

As I looked out over the beauty and calmness of the yellow sea, I sensed a tender breeze all around me, and it whispered to me softly. I, then felt even more confident. As I got stronger and stronger, I turned around. I traced my tracks, and went up to my room. It had been a crushing twenty-eight hour day. I had had little food and no rest, and I had no job. Yet, I believed God would keep a place for me to go if I did get some rest. But peaceful rest would not come. I was haunted by that F-4 fighter jet's fuel system not feeding properly, and we almost lost his generation points.

Knowing that some might have career issues after that. It was not good. But Monday morning did come, and after having been fired, I knew I needed to be on leave, in the hospital or at work-somewhere. Otherwise, I would be (AWOL), absent without official leave. But I wasn't on leave, I wasn't sick, and I had no job to go to. So to dispel any hint of being AWOL, I reported to my Squadron Commander's office. I couldn't see him right away. I waited and waited, but he was busy. My Squadron Commander was so busy, that it was almost impossible for me to see him any time soon. Therefore, I communicated with him through his secretary, a Korean lady, by hand written notes. For about two weeks, I left notes with the secretary, indicating my exact location, and that I was at my Commander's disposal any time, at his convenience.

The secretary understood everything. She acted with solid resolve, as my voice to my commander. In the meantime, I searched, and I read everything about the air force that was available to me.

When I was able to speak to my Squadron Commander, he was open, he was humble, and he was honest with me. He told me that we cut it too close during the exercise. And because there were mitigating circumstances, some people were spared.

"Even though we passed, we had to show some corrective action." He said.

They looked at careers very closely to determine who would suffer the least if there was corrective action taken.

"In view of your position to the mission that night, and the career progression you have made, with the possibility of being at the top of your career (E-9) with less than twenty years of service, your career would be one of the least damaged, if damaged at all."

At that very moment, I thought, "sacrificed?" And, yes, I was sacrificed. I took another one for the team. It was another lesson. But God is faithful. He kept a place for me to go to work. My Squadron Commander reinstated me to my job. He knew that professionalism and excellence would prevail if I went back there, because the officer in charge and I were professionals. We had worked on many projects together. He was an excellent manager, as I tried to be. We roamed the flight line and the fuel farms together, making inspections, and talking to the troops.

He was a great morale booster and team builder, as I was. We often rode our bikes to work, side by side. And, he played a commendable second base on the section's softball team that I coached that summer. It was obvious that there was harmony in the work place, but things happen. The pressure of the no notice inspection, and me getting fired after the inspection was just one of those unfortunate things that happen. Yes, things happen. But, mind you, certain shockers can adversely affect one's health. If you're not strong, adversity could affect one's mental health. So, by all means, take care of your mental health. It's an unparalleled gift of God.

When you have done everything in your power to get a work done, and you can't get it done, if its causing you unsafe anxiety issues, you have to let it go. So, shake it loose and let it fall. Let it lie for a season, maybe forever. Move on with your life in an excellent way. The remainder of my remote tour at Kunsan AFB, Korea went outstandingly well. I returned home in early February 1980, and made arrangements for my wife to join me at Maxwell Air Force base, Montgomery, Alabama. Maxwell was the perfect assignment for personnel in my career field; especially if you preferred a lighter work environment. Maxwell's flying mission was minimum, personnel were few. Things ran smoothly. The assignment clearly didn't need a Senior Master sergeant as superintendent. The reason they wanted me at Maxwell, was, they had me figured to become an officer. At least, that's the way I under stood it. My immediate chain of command thought it would be appropriate for me to start in a small place.

"You've got the savvy to be a commissioned officer," they told me. I appreciated the compliment and their confidence in my leadership ability, but I wasn't very likely to become a commissioned officer because I was already thirty-nine years old. I believe thirty-four years of age is the cut off for making the transition from non-commissioned officer to commissioned officer. It was an excellent idea though. Maybe someone thought that I would make an excellent foreign affairs negotiating officer. Maybe, they thought I'd make a great negotiator for the world's most sought after, and the forever political resource, that being petroleum products.

I continued to work diligently in my assignment, but a radical change of events occurred. My nine skill level was reduced to a seven skill level. The idea of me becoming an officer, just wasn't factual, under the circumstances. These issues were cause for concern. I accessed my chain of command trying to get relieved from Maxwell, but nothing happened. Then, at my, request, an appointment with the chaplain was made for me, for my peace of mind. This felt so dysfunctional. Even a chaplain's assistant would have been fine, anyone.

But, to my surprise, my appointment was with a 06, a full bird colonel. Can you believe that? He may have been the regional chaplain. After the colonel and I talked for a few moments, he excused himself and went into another room and answered the telephone. When he returned, he just said to me, they want you to become an officer. If you don't want to become an officer, you might as well start preparing to become a civilian, or something to that effect.

This was a stoic ending to my conversation with the colonel, the man of God. But then, I can't really say that it was a stoic ending because I acted with passion. When I left that office, I was totally confused. I was sweating and I was shaking like a TRANS-AM on cheap gas. Stoic, according to Zeno's Greek school of philosophy, holds that "human beings should be free from passion and calmly accept all occurrences as the unavoidable result of divine will." So then, maybe, it was just another painful trial to endure. If you can endure your trials, it will increase your faith. That's what they tell me. That's what they say.

Even though confused, I waited. I waited because I totally believed in the U.S. Air Force and my leaders. I was humble, honest, and never insubordinate while I waited. After ten months, I was yet working in a position below my lawfully achieved nine skill level. This was a sign of a sure career breaker. I could have been facing forced retirement for in competence, if I didn't fight. To fight meant speaking to someone, but I had no one else to speak to. I don't believe anyone had acted intentionally, in anyway, to confuse,or betray me. But, there again, I may have been facing forced retirement.

It could have been, that we all were just grasping after the wind, while looking for someone to lean on. What I didn't understand about the small place where I found myself, was, that it was a place of perfecting. I needed to stay there until God had made me strong enough, wise enough, and flexible enough to successfully manage the very, very large place that he had predestined for me to go. So I just had to lean on him. My faith said wait on the Lord because he knows how to get his children's attention, and in his own unique way.

He got Moses attention by speaking to him from within a burning bush, and the bush was not consumed. Exodus 3–4. He got Balaam's attention through the voice of a talking donkey, Numbers 22:22–30. And God got Samuels attention by calling his name, Samuel, Samuel, four times. See 1st Samuel, 3:1–10. When God's message is urgent, and we cannot afford to miss it, he puts us in such an uncompromising position, that we just cannot miss his voice. Then I said, surely, the Lord will speak to me if it pleases him to speak to me. I heard of a man that was in a small place, but he loved God with all his heart and all his soul and all of his mind, as I did. God took that man out of that small place, and put him in a very large place. And I said, surely, he would do the same for me if I would just wait on his will, and his predetermination for me.

26

God's Manifest, Assignment to Bentwaters, AB England

I began to see God's will for me start to manifest its self when I surprisingly received a survey from Norton Air Force Base, San Bernardino, California. The survey specifically asked, if I were working in a skill level that supported my rank. I informed my supervisor about the survey. Then I replied with the appropriate answers. After I did this, I started receiving quiet prompts about what to do. The first prompt I received was to put away my work and go for a walk. But the prompter failed to tell me which way or where to go. So I put away my work, and walked out to my black and gold, 6.6 liter, four-speed TRANS-AM. But I quickly turned down that idea, saying, "where do I go from here?" Because the (6.6) may have turned up instant trouble.

The second prompt that I received was about one week later. This prompt was much like the first, not telling me which way or where to go. So I stopped what I was doing, and I walked to the front of the building, up to the fuels control center. I signed out, and reported out. Then I walked down the perimeter of the flight line, past the Civil Air Patrol (CAP) office, and on down to the Aero Club. I walked into the Aero Club's office for no pre-planned purpose at all. The Aero Club supervisor fondly greeted me. He was friendly, and he was exceedingly excited about the Aero Club's flying program. He also was very skillful at judging, and selecting candidates who had excellent potential to learn to fly. He judged me as such. I had an informed, but brief visit with the supervisor. And then I left, because I had to move along. I had an open invitation to return for flight training.

Flexing my lunch break, whenever possible, I returned. And, overtime, we covered the basics of flying, safety, attention to detail, etc. We also covered pre-flight and post-flight procedures, which were easy, since I had worked around aircraft most of my military career. When the basic flying training was satisfactorily completed, the Aero Club supervisor assigned me an airplane to train in, and an instructor pilot. My assigned airplane was a Cessna PA-140. The PA-140 was a better handler and a smoother ride than other Cessna's due to the under body wing configuration, according to the Aero Club supervisor. My instructor was an army captain, who was an experienced pilot, and an excellent training instructor. Now, I've got an airplane, I've got an instructor, I just needed training time.

I needed to train during my lunch break, out of courtesy to my job and my supervisor. I cleared every procedure through my supervisor, a young, Air Force 1st lieutenant. It was fine with her, as she was perfect with the entire process. My wife was fine with my flying process as well, but she politely turned down every offer to come fly with me, opting to watch from the safety of the ground.

When my instructor and I flew, we flew by landmarks. There was a big silo for storing hay, corn, and soybeans. There was a red barn, cow pastures, red farmland, the Alabama River, and such along our route. We always flew down toward Mississippi and back, safely. I was a safe flyer, and even though I was safe, my instructor was constantly reminding me to watch out for birds, and avoid bird strikes because severe air mishaps are caused by them. I got it. I got our flight plan too.

On or about our fifth flight, I also got that feeling. You know how you get a feeling that things aren't going to go just like they ought, some days. You know, how you get that condition that starts down in your naval area, and it creeps slowly up past your diaphragm, on into your chest? When you feel that way, you know something is going to haunt you. But you say, my countenance is good. I can deal with it. Or you may say, what in the world have I done wrong? Well, that's exactly how I felt that day, as my flight instructor and I flew along, discussing our flight plan.

We had a lot going on that day. We were to fly directly above the Alabama river for a short distance, just to get the effects that the river's currents had on a small air plane in flight. Our, flight plan also had us discussing stacking and practicing *touch and go's*.

Stacking: A stack is a fixed circling pattern in which aircraft fly while they wait to land. When there is a build-up of airplanes waiting to land, Air Traffic Control (ATC) must ensure that there is a safe gap between each airplane as they come in to land. To achieve this, aircraft will sometimes circle around in a stack until the air traffic controllers are able to fit them into the landing pattern. When the lead airplane in the bottom stack is approved to land, it drops out of the stack and another aircraft takes its place. This process continues until all the stacks are depleted, and all the aircraft have safely landed.

Touch and Go: Touch and go practice provides the advanced student and certified pilot technique for an emergency go-around should he detect a hazard after touching down, such as an animal or other airplane on the run way. Touch and goes also speed the process of learning to land an airplane by compressing more landings into the typical flight lesson. This process requires a pilot, after doing all the landing safety checks, to touch down, and roll a short distance.

Then increase engine power, and regain altitude, and go around again. I was excited about these *touch and go's* as we returned to Maxwell from our heading down toward Mississippi. Maxwell tower cleared us to shoot some landings or *touch and go's*. I hoped that nothing would take my attention away from getting these carefully planned touch and goes right. No birds, no distractions, no nothing. Who would want to distract someone who's trying to land an air aircraft? But I had that feeling. I just had that feeling that something odd was going to happen. I made a low approach, and my instructor asked me to pick a spot where I wanted to touch down when I came back around. He approved the spot. I was in harmony with all of my senses, including perfect hearing over the aircraft noise.

When I came back around and was descending for my first touch and go, something knocked me on my right shoulder. It hit me so hard that I lost concentration. And I looked back. When I looked back, a gentle voice spoke to me. It spoke two words.

The voice spoke these two words to me. "Call Randolph." My instructor quickly got me back on track by calling, "Ralph!Ralph! You are going to miss your spot, pull up and go around again."

Maxwell tower cleared us to do another go around. This time we landed and gave way to approaching air traffic. We taxied the PA-140 to the hanger, and did a post flight inspection. Then my training instructor, the Aero Club, supervisor, and I, bade one another farewell. And I, thus suspended my flying training. I had heard from the one whom I had been waiting so long to hear from. It had to have been God who spoke these two words, to me, "Call Randolph when I was landing that aircraft.

I was for certain in an unfamiliar position. A command to call *Randolph* was unclear to me. I was neither at odds with, nor was I social with anyone named *Randolph*. I didn't dare call Willie *Randolph*, the baseball player. I didn't know him. I had merely heard that he was an upstanding citizen and a superior second base man for the big hitting New York Yankees.

But what I did learn upon further inquiry was that, the *Randolph* in question, was Randolph Air Force Base, located near Sa -Antonio, Texas. That's where Senior Non-Commissioned officer's records are maintained. I was commanded by the voice to call there for assistance to get me to the place that had been predestined for me to go. So I called *Randolph*. And when I did, I asked the records specialist if he could help me to get reassigned. I warned the records specialist up front that I may have had a major set back to my records because of what happened in Korea. I also informed him that my skill level had been downgraded at Maxwell, from a nine to a seven.

The records specialist needed about ten working days to check things out.

When he returned my call, he reported that, "they didn't hurt you in Korea. With your records, you can go anywhere in the world you want to go," he said.

I would have chosen to go to Japan, Spain, or back to Germany, or Ramey Air Force Base, Puerto Rico. But Ramey was closed. And the other popular assignments were already filled to six years and beyond by senior enlisted staff in my career field.

But he did have a Chief's (E-9) position open in England. It was a tough assignment to fill, because of its complexity, size, and its exceeding heavy responsibilities. The E-9's were in a position that they could retire if he pressed them too much. Since I was an E-8 and imminently qualified, the records specialist assured me that if I would take the assignment for him, he could have me out of Maxwell within two months. I leaped at the opportunity because I was predestined to go there, and I had spent my time in preparation for the assignment. Being reassigned weighs on a soul because you get to know people and people get to know you, and then you have to leave them behind. Even though, sometimes, it may have been touch and go at Maxwell, we had a mutual and a kind respect for each other.

The touchy situations were all about a refining process that no one understood. Not even I understood it. Plus, it was about total career responsibility. Now, it is down to two months to get things done. Barbara and I sold our home two weeks before departing Maxwell AFB for a net profit of $10,000.00 dollars. While getting ever thing else done, i.e., administratively cleaning the base and attending social gatherings, we were consumed with taking the long trip north, from Montgomery, Alabama to Portsmouth, New Hampshire. We said our good-byes, and traveling began. Our traveling means and companions were a Trans-Am, a Pontiac Grandville, and a Toyota Starlet, our Heavenly Father, plus two dogs, Brandy and Ginger. I hooked on to the Trans-Am with the Grandville, and Barbara and the dogs had charge of the Starlet.

We drove to Cartersville, Georgia to visit my family before going overseas. After a few days visit, we drove to Goldsboro, North Carolina to visit my wife's family. And from Goldsboro, we continued on up to Bayonne, New Jersey to (R.O.N.) rest overnight, and ship the starlet to England the next morning. After that, we continued on North to New Haven, Connecticut where we visited more of Barbara's family.

Then she and I drove with the dogs on home to Portsmouth, New Hampshire with the Trans-Am still hooked on. It felt peaceful and relaxing to be home for a few days before continuing on our journey to England. There was time enough to get the boys, Reggie and Carl, who were a couple of years or so out of high school prepared the responsibilities as keepers of the house, the three years of our absence would fall to them. I also had time to try to visualize what my new assignment would be like. And then my welcoming letter caught up with me. The initial greeting of the welcoming letter read in part, "I'm taking this opportunity to welcome you to the Fuels Management Branch of the 81st Supply Squadron. We support the 81st Tactical Fighter wing, home of the A10 Thunder Bolt II, and the largest fighter wing in the Air Force, and possibly the world."

The letter went on to mention the numerous North Atlantic Treaty Organization (NATO) aircraft serviced by our people every day.

Our responsibilities to the twin bases, Royal Air Force (RAF) Bentwaters, and RAF Woodbridge, the location of the refueling hot pad, where a percentage of the A10's refueled without ever completely shutting down their engines; the first, and only in the United Kingdom. The Forward Operating Locations (FOL's) in West Germany and mobility support to NATO were mentioned as being an important part of our scope of responsibilities. All this and more were enough for me to get excited about. I, again, recalled some of the words my mother uttered to me back in chapter eleven, when I was leaving home at age sixteen, "if you stay close to the umbilical card that fed you, you will go places and do things that are uncommon to lowly people."

I serviced B52's for action in the Mutually Assured Destruction (MAD) phase of the cold war in the early 1960's, and I survived the contagiously saddening Vietnam War. By much grace and favor, I was handpicked and security cleared as a refueling supervisor for Air Force One, the most supreme, and the most highly secured air craft in the universe.

I raised two sons and tutored them and other young boys to play baseball at the world level. I have always tried to stay close to the umbilical cord that fed me. And by holding on tight, when I was about to be written off down at Maxwell, God's hand of favor was turned toward me. And now, I am about to embark upon a journey that will take me so many lonely, yet joyful miles away from home where I will be assigned as Fuels Superintendent that will support the largest Tactical Fighter Wing in the Air Force, and possibly the world. That's what God' will do for you, if you will just trust him. The umbilical cord, and my maker, if my maker stays with me, I shall get my job done; I shall get it done in my, lifetime even, if it's just before dawn. Before dawn, and time was yet on my side, but time was drawing near to the time to continue the journey toward Europe.

I had been granted concurrent travel, meaning that my wife could travel right by my side. Before we left, we prayed that God would be the watchman and the keeper of the boys, the dogs, and the house that we left for them. We prayed to God, that excellent character, would define the boys as he provided for their every Christly need while we were away.

We gathered our basic necessities, we said good-bye, and we boarded a jet plane out of Boston.

Within a few hours, we had crossed the Atlantic Ocean. My wife and I arrived at Bentwaters, AFB, England, in late May or early June 1981 where we were cheerfully greeted.

27

Enthusiasm in England

There was so much enthusiasm, that during in processing, some of the young airmen would find ways to stop by the office to get a sneak peek, and say hi to their new leader before I had a chance to formally greet them all. There were eighty-five to one hundred personnel assigned to Bentwaters–Woodbridge Fuels Management. They were mostly very young, eighteen to their mid-twenties in age, maybe. I felt that my strong faith, and my many years of experience made me a competent, leader for them. But I wanted to be more than just a leader. I wanted to be trustworthy and involved in their cares. I desired also to be a joy to follow. And I think they knew that. And of course, there were older first line supervisors and middle managers who were avid supporters of the aircraft flying mission and the young enthusiastic troops. And speaking of enthusiasm, there was another kind of enthusiasm raging in England when my wife and I arrived.

The Royals and much of the world excitedly and enthusiastically awaited the wedding of Charles, Prince of Whales, and Lady Diana Spencer. The wedding took place on Wednesday, 29 July 1981 at St. Paul's Cathedral, London, United Kingdom. This marriage was widely billed as a "fairytale wedding" and the "wedding of the century." It was a privilege to have been so close to such noble history in the making.

While I thoroughly appreciated and enjoyed the public's contagious enthusiasm about the royal couple, I was busy getting processed in. During in processing, my wife and I moved into the Quonset huts on Bentwaters Air Force Base, temporarily. Then we moved to Saxmundham, a small market town in Suffolk, England. Its setting is about eleven miles south East of Benwaters AFB, eighteen miles North East of Ipswich, and five miles west of the coast of the North Sea, at Sizewell. The military housing community there presented with a pleasant and safe living environment. Our plans were to buy new European furniture, but when some of the military wives taught Barbara how to be successful at the auctions, she changed her mind. She took advantage of the auction specials instead. What's more, she had some cash left over to do what women do with money, save a little, and spend a lot!

28
Learning the Mission of the 81st

Also, during in processing, I was doing lots of listening and studying the role of the Tactical Air Command in Europe, and how the 81st TFW contributed to that discipline. I was also strategizing to see how we at fuels could best match up and stay ahead of mission requirements. I learned that tactical air power here had three classic missions, basically as elsewhere. They were: first, interdiction (slowing down or stopping the enemy); second, air-superiority (being the best fighters in the air); and third, close air support. "For many years in the past, the F4 Phantom II did all of these things. Then the F-111 Ardvark was employed to do a lot of the interdiction. Then the F-15 Strike Eagle came on board with the U.S. Air Forces in Europe as air superiority specialists. There was still room for the F-4 as well as the F-16 fighting Falcon to play a role. And now the A-10 Thunder bolt II has picked up the close air support specialty." The F-16 replaced the F-4. The Navy's F14 Tom Cat pilots had a role in training the A-10 pilots for their new combat role.

The A-10 is an excellent asset that was conceived during the Vietnam War. It came on board with the 81st as an excellent, reliable, and versatile attack fighter in early 1979. It is so versatile that it can come in at tree top level and protect the troops on the ground. The A-10's basic weapon is the 30-millimeter (mm) Gatlin gun, known as tank killers, but the A-10 can do much more. Because of its lethality and the A10's low speed, the pilot can find, track, and kill a tank without over flying it. That's a real advantage to any pilot in a high threat environment. In a fast mover, you can't identify your target and get set up in one pass-you're simply moving too fast. But the A-10 is just like a kid throwing rocks at a rattlesnake, you stay out of his reach and throw those 30 mm rocks until he's no longer a threat. The A-10's were to perform most of their tactical work in the Federal Republic of Germany from four forward operating locations FOL's). And they were to do rearward maintenance at Bent-waters and Woodbridge Air Force bases in England.

The Fuels Management Branch had its work cut out for it. The 81st TFW beamed with six Squadrons, 117 A-10A aircraft, making it the biggest wing in the USAF. The 67th Aerospace Rescue and Recovery Squadron (ARRS), stationed at RAF Woodbridge was the world's largest rescue squadron.

It was charged with saving lives and aiding the injured in an area that stretches from the North Pole to South Africa and from the mid-Atlantic to the borders of Burma, an area consisting of literally millions of square miles. This Squadron flew HC-130 "Hercules" and HH-53 "Super Jolly Green Giant" helicopters. Whether destroying enemy armor or coming to the aid of a downed pilot, these missions wouldn't have been possible without adequate fuels support. Our fuels people realized the importance of their job and so strived to provide the best service possible both at the main bases and while TDY at our FOLs in Germany, and any other location throughout NATO, Aviano, Italy, Denmark, Turkey, and other countries.

To have so many young people in so many different places and expect them to perform well, required a great deal of trust and allegiance. Character was a big part of it, but building character was not really a problem because we had excellent people. The youngsters cherished traveling, most of them. So, if any of them were having character issues, we helped them get back on track, so they could hold on to the privilege.

To build trust and allegiance, we structured our home teams and TDY (Mobility) teams so that no one could lord it over on another. We assured our people that we would stand by them in times of trouble and uncertainness. We trained hard. We trained very hard. Safety was the first and the last word. When people know without a doubt, what they are doing, it builds confidence. With safety, knowledge, and confidence, you can cut your losses to a bare minimum, and turn them into quality gains.

Our people were excellent receptors of these concepts. Safety, knowledge, confidence, hard work, and character were hot angles to us getting through it all. In the absence of both a captain and a chief master sergeant, we operated with junior officers. I was, therefore, required to travel out of country, as a negotiator, coordinator, and writer for the Joint Support (JSP) Site Survey and Host Nation Support Model Study Team. This position came with the territory of being fuels superintendent with the 81st TFW, at the time.

The 81st needed surety that the Host Nation, Germany, would be joint supporters of the resources for the new concept of war planning that the A-10 presented. The team negotiated for air space, aircraft parking space, munitions storage space, mortuary service, transportation, food service, petroleum products and any other resource necessary to fight a war and win.

My primary role on the team was negotiating for petroleum products, a must asset for every one to have. It was a committed effort, and it was all about aircraft ground support. I was committed to becoming the best aircraft ground support airman I could be when I realized that I probably would not become a pilot. As mentioned earlier, I got a slow start in education because working on the farm consumed so much of my school time and prevented me from getting a good jump toward a quality early education. It was heartbreak hill, but I used my high school education, military training, to include military academies, and leadership schools, plus I took college courses to help me to keep up.

My home training played a positive role as well. I never thought that even one drop of my sweat, while staying out of school and doing hard work on the farm, was leading me to anything but another cotton field or one more heart break hill. Though, in reality, the hard farm work, Gods favor, traveling rocky, dusty, winding roads, and climbing those high mountains was helping to construct me to help a nation. It was helping me to help our great nation and its allies to end a war; a war that had been posturing for forty-two years or more, the cold war.

Traveling, writing, and negotiating with the German Officers enabled me to have a role in this. It was a truly supreme experience for me. However, there was but one left turn. I had to leave my wife alone in England, a place perceived to have had ghost sightings, and where many ghost stories were told. My wife was terrified of ghost, but she understood my having to leave her alone some time. I think she was super naturally protected from the fear of ghost; at least while I was away. Because she didn't know that there was possibly, a presence in the house.

You could hear footsteps on the stairs when you were in our house alone at night. Neither did she know that the bedroom ceiling light did crazy things, and the curtains swayed angrily sometimes even with the windows closed. My wife feeling safe while I was away helped me to do my job without interruption! For this, I'm forever grateful to my wife and to the heavens, I'm very thankful. You know?But the mission called for mobility.

Our son, Carl, experienced the footsteps on the stairway and the suspicious curtain movement when he and our son, Reggie, visited us in 1983.

29
Traveling and Writing

Not much gets done when you are standing still. We had to keep moving to get from England to Germany and all the FOLs. Our basic transportation was by C-130 Hercules transport aircraft, known by some GI's as "Fat Albert." "Fat Albert," made his rounds to all the FOLs three times a week. Military travelers in need of a ride, we just climbed aboard, and sat among whatever cargo that needed to be transported that day, whether a 30mm Gatlin gun, assembly, pickup truck, a weapons jammer, big truck tires, etc. And if that wasn't exciting enough, sometimes, if you were already in country and needed to get ahead of "Fat Albert," catching the German train at night was an option. However, though, no military uniforms.

On one occasion, two of our troops and I had traveled much of the night by train until daybreak. Then we caught a taxi to get on out to our final destination. It was drizzling rain, and the highway was slippery. Our taxi driver was impatient and in a hurry. I do believe we were traveling with a hedge of protection around us that morning to save us from the grievous finality of death, because as we were sitting at the tail end of a traffic jam; a big truck topped the hill. He was traveling too fast to stop. Our impatient but alert driver saw the truck in his rear view mirror, and he instantly moved to the shoulder of the road and drove forward a few car lengths. We were lucky, very lucky.

But the lady in the car that had been just ahead of us was not quite so lucky. Her car took the full impact of that big truck. Her car hit other cars, and the woman ended up on the opposite side of the highway, trapped in her woefully mangled, and smoldering vehicle. She needed immediate help. Some German men rushed to aid her, but they soon returned to their places. Why did they leave her? I asked the wind. It could have been them. It could have been anyone needing help. It could have been me. These hands of mine desperately wanted to help. I was just passing through. Yet, I tried to aid her.

And just like the German men, I was unable to do anything to help. The woman's feet were pinned down under the foot pedals. Her face lay badly lacerated and bleeding on the twisted steering wheel. And she was moaning softly, screaming, I reckon. But only muffled words that were past understanding would come out. She was in pain, so much pain that it touched my heart, and it rocked my pericardium sac. The pericardium sac is a double walled sac that houses the heart and the roots of the great vessels, and it was past understanding that I was unable to help. Plus, I had to leave that innocent human being in such a poor and pitiful condition. But, my taxi was waiting. He was blowing his horn.

I, therefore, gave her my best prayer; and I left her in the healing hands of the Lord. The helping hands of the rescue people were in sight. The sight of me having been just passing through was like being out there on the pain of the cold, cold wind. The pain that the poor woman bore may have been my pain to bear. I never learned the official end of the matter. I was just out there on the wind. And when you are out there on the wind, doing a job you've been chosen and constructed to do, there will surely be anxious moments. But you go on. You go on because you and others are accountable for the safety, security and the peace of the people about the world.

Anxious moments, you say? Well, it was around the first of December 1981, we were in flight on a C-130 from Bentwaters AFB, England, with the Joint Support Plans (JSP) team. Our travel order was TA-2775. Our objective was to perform a JSP Site Survey and Host Nation Support Model Study at OTU 10 Jever German Air Base, Germany. We were in search of a suitable place to support additional personnel and equipment, and to employ the A-10 for its ability to match up with, and defeat the most severe threats as posed by the massive imbalance of armor between the Warsaw Pact and NATO countries. It was very urgent that we get on the ground and get to work without delay- if possible.

We were way up there in North East Germany. Up there near the busiest artificial (man made) water way in the world, the Kiel Canal. The

Kiel Canal also connects the North Sea and the Baltic Sea. (A lot of water)! Siberia, Russia, and the Baltic countries frequent those waters. And it gets down right foggy up there. The fog gets so dense, that sometimes, it makes landing very difficult to impossible. We made several attempts to land at Jever that afternoon, but the intense fog would not give. So we climbed up over the stuff, and circled for hours it seemed.

Just one crack in the ceiling (a hint of light) realizing the nature of the mission, our pilots decided to give landing one more try. If we could find that one crack in the ceiling, we were going in. As we were trying to land, we were dropping into darkness so rapidly, that it was like dropping into a dark sack that was trying to protect something, like the pericardium sac protects the heart. You won't find a crack in the pericardium sac, though. You have to pierce it. And when you pierce the pericardium sac, you get blood and water. (I'll just leave the pericardial fluid the pericardium sac, and the pericardial cavity for the biblical ministers to correlate with the piercing of Jesus). John 19-34

To avoid the blood and water experience, our excellent Air Force pilots nosed that C-130 up, and soared back toward England. And as we flew, my trembling heart resettled in its pericardium sac. We had just experienced another contagiously anxious moment. But it was an equally proud moment when we landed at RAF Mildenhall, England. We rested overnight (RON) there. Meanwhile, our Host Nation counter parts understandably awaited, our, return to North East, Germany the following day.

We landed with little resistance from the fog this time. And over time, using humility, meekness, and diplomacy, the JSP team got its job done successfully. And during the following year, the monumental task of finalizing the Joint Support Plans (JSPs) for four Forward Operating Locations (FOL) and two Co-located Operating Bases was completed. These complex JSPs clearly defined the responsibilities, requirements, and shortfalls of the United States Air Force and the other North Atlantic Treaty Organization (NATO) country. It was just one of many initiatives of the 81st TFW that undoubtedly helped to end the cold war.

30

Recognition And Loss

The 81st TFW flew and trained the way it would fly and fight if necessary. It set three consecutive world records for the most sorties flown in a fourteen- hour period for a single tactical fighter wing for1981, 1982, and 1983, and it achieved a USAF peace time flying record of 53,000 hours in 1982. This helped the Wing to win the coveted Daedalian Trophy for best in maintenance. Every organization contributed. Such contributions influenced the closing of the cold war. The loyalty and dedication to the United States Air Force mission, from the most junior to the most senior fuels personnel assigned, insured safe and timely wing A10 fuels support for these phenomenal accomplishments.

There was much recognition for all the support units, especially the Fuels Branch and its people. Such as the coveted Golden Drum award for Third Air Force, three times. The Golden Drum Award is an arm of the American Petroleum Institute (API), Fuels Superintendent of the year, 1981, 1982, and 1983 for Third Air Force. Some of our fuels people were recognized as best in the Air Force for different rank structures. We were a close-knit group who was stirred if even one of us was hurting. Not to think of losing one. However, though, we did lose one of our, very finest young airmen. We lost him to the finality of death in 1984. His privately owned vehicle went out of control on a small curve and over turned. No one understood it, as he was within the limits of all driving safety standards.

Since we were such a close-knit group, the base chaplain recommended that someone who worked with the young airman, officiate his funeral. The lot fell to the leader to perform this incredibly responsible, and somber task. There had been so many questions, questions of why such a good person? Why such a contributor to what is right? Why so young? So in the closing remarks of his eulogy, I, as their leader, said something to this effect, "his loss is beyond man's understanding. And like you, I have questions. But I take comfort in knowing that every matter, no matter how tragic, every decision has been touched by the loving hands of God. Yes, I have questions. But who am I to question God's authority"? In spirit, everyone knew that our parted beloved friend would want us to be safe and comforted. Yet, everyone went about grieving in his or her own special way.

In your own special way, you feel so uncertain some times. You look around you, and try to understand who has been holding on to you and leading you for so long. Sometimes you look around to see if you have given every challenge you faced -your very, very best. Have you, given it all of your caring heart? And if something didn't work out just right, how would you fix it, if you had a chance to do it all over again? But looking around, and looking back, and looking forward, I hope the voice that I followed (God's voices) can deal peacefully with my efforts while stationed with the 81st TFW, because I left it all in His hands, and on the flight line. It was a memorable education dealing with and learning about the people and the wide spread-complex Air Force mission here. You have to perform the Air Force mission, and you have to perform your role in it, powerfully well. No question? Does it touch you? You know? Furthermore, the year of manufacturing the time after regular duty hours to coach the Bentwaters Phantoms varsity baseball team, who played in the United Kingdom League. I learned so much about myself. I'm yet evolving from the experience. I also learned volumes about how participation in athletic activities correlates so closely with dealing with people, and the highs and lows of daily living.

Then to, when looking back, I always think of the little children, the fourth, and fifth graders whom I taught in Sunday school at Bentwaters. Gosh, those children were so brilliant! One Sunday, I didn't quite have their Sunday school lesson prepared. And I told them that I had been preparing a commanders briefing instead, which I had been. The children respectively informed me that their Sunday school lesson was just as important as a Commanders briefing. God bless the children; because there are some things he has not shown them yet! But they were kind. They let me off the hook because some of their dads were commanders.

And some of their parents were, otherwise, powerful and diligent men and women. Therefore, we all prospered in the name of Jesus, as the courageous children and I worked the lesson out together.

Things always work out, if it's meant to be. If it's God inspired. No matter how small or great the task. I felt so worthy at RAF Bentwaters-RAF Woodbridge as Fuels Superintendent for the largest Tactical Fighter Wing in the world. It came naturally. Even though it was such a potentially stressful place, and it was so jet inspired busy. I knew I couldn't have done it alone. So I prayed a lot. And there was a lot of delegation of authority. And considering the bumpy roads, and heartbreak hills of Kunsan AFB, Korea and Maxwell AFB, Alabama, I have conceded them to have been the unavoidable results of divine will.

31

One Reassignment-A Four Star's Approval - Retirement

Before I completed my standard three-year accompanied tour in my present assignment, there was talk that I would be getting promoted to Chief Master Sergeant. Chief, to some, is the most prestigious rank in the U.S. Air Force. It has its reasons. Some of the young troops would contagiously utter, "you are going to be the Chief Master of the Air Force some, day." But I knew that the competiveness in many cases, for promotion to chief, without question, would require a four-star general's endorsements. Getting a four-star's blessing was no easy task. Especially having been so far geographically removed from a four star. But if this were to happen, it would have to happen at my new assignment back in the states. I was reassigned to the 380th Bombardment Wing, Strategic Air Command (SAC) Plattsburgh AFB, New York, in July 1984.

Your local commanders paved the way to higher authority for you if you were in the right standing with them. SAC had power and influence, and if you didn't know the power and influence of SAC, back then, you didn't know SAC. As far as I needed a four-star general's endorsements to elevate me to the rank of chief master sergeant, a four- tar general came to my duty section at Plattsburg AFB, and shook my hand. Was God up to something? God is always up to something. But the general was on base for much, much bigger business. Now, let me qualify that handshake.

At my duty section, we had an experienced officer in charge. He was a senior captain, and that was a good thing. He was so affluent in dealing with the various commanders, executive staff officers, and logistics. Therefore, I could concentrate on the enlisted personnel's career progression, personnel morale maintenance, and the flying mission. But this soon took a different course. On reporting to my Squadron Commander, a Lieutenant Colonel, (05), and my, Resource Management Commander, (RM), a full bird Colonel, (06). They assured me of their- confidence in me as Fuels Superintendent.

Then, they informed me that we would be losing our captain. We would be losing him for an extended period of time. The captain was up for promotion to Major (04), but he needed to catch up on some mandatory military education first. A lot of activity was expected on the base during the captain's absence. The periodic Operational Readiness Inspection (ORI) and the Inspector General (IG) would come due while the captain was away. Therefore, my commanders looked to me for the overall management of my duty section. Realizing if God's hand stayed on me, as so many times before, I would be able and accountable to carry out my duties.

We were locked up in support of those meticulous and swift nuclear carrying bombers, and those mission essential air to air refueling flight-extending tankers. Even though we were, I informed my Commanders that I would do everything within my power to help elevate the high standards of the mission, and I gladly took full responsibility for the Fuels account, and I signed for it. The assigned Master Sergeants and I knew that we had a great challenge ahead of us. So we put our heads together. And we brought all of the troops plus the secretary on board with us. And the attitude of the whole group was positive. It was all about performing the mission safely, timely, and excellently. We also labored on helping get the captain promoted, taking care of each other, and not embarrassing anyone.

By the time the captain returned, we had achieved an excellent, and the overall highest rating on the Operational Readiness Inspection (ORI), and the Inspector General (IG), the Fuels Management Branch had received in many, many years. People were impressed. People were so impressed that a four-star General was alerted. General Bennie Luke Davis, the Strategic Air Command (SAC) Commander, came to our duty section. He toured the facilities and thanked personnel for outstanding aircraft fuel support, and maintaining combat readiness at Air Force's highest tradition; a job well done. With this level of recognition, it goes without saying the captain received his promotion to Major (04)

When the General shook my hand, he looked upon me with kindness, mercy, understanding, and with godly favor in his eyes. I, therefore knew, the General knew, that he was the Spirit of Wisdom, and of uncontested power, and authority to affect my promotion to perhaps the most prestigious rank in the US Air Force, Chief Master Sergeant, E-9. Why is Chief master sergeant such a prestigious milestone to reach? Chiefs are in the top one percent of all enlisted Air Force personnel. And as such, the most junior airman, to the most senior generals are inclined to listen to the wisdom of a Chief. To accept chief, I would have been mandated to stay an additional two or more years. This was easily doable. But my family life took a crushing left turn. My son was in college in Boston and was trying to help maintain our home in Portsmouth, New Hampshire. He was at his wits end.

Then my wife's mother suffered her third stroke, which paralyzed her on one side. And she needed family help. My wife, being the oldest of three daughters, became the natural choice to help her mother. We drove from Plattsburgh AFB, NY to Rocky Mount, North Carolina and picked my wife's mother up. We brought her to our home in Portsmouth, NH, to take care of her.

Taking care of the sick, in this case, was too much of a job for one person. Consequently, after much consideration, it appeared that I would need to retire to help the sick and to hold my family together. In further study, I considered the fact that the Air Force was continually training under studies to fill the boots of departed personnel. So I knew the air force would be just fine without me, but there was no one to fill my boots at home. My commanders understood my situation. And yet they supported me to stay. But they finally conceded that, "surely, there's life after the Air Force." I, therefore, looked past my own desires, and looked toward the needs of others.

I left the potentially assured promotion on the table to fulfill a calling, a calling to touch and help nurture the disabled, and to secure my family. I retired. In my head, it was a tough decision. But in my heart, it was the right decision. Things happen. Things happen for a reason, I reckon.

Having had the opportunity to serve this great nation of ours and the world from July 19, 1961 to January 1, 1986 was a time of joy, patriotism, and sacrifice. Many unusual opportunities, not often afforded to the lowly, were set at the feet of this lowly one. I hope I pleased God and man, by doing the right thing with those opportunities. It was a great honor to serve. Looking back, my stoic brown eyes are often filled with joyous dampness, when I think of all the support I received from God's hands, and from the hands of man while trying to fulfill my dream. My dream was to be a follower of Christ, and to be the best aircraft ground support airman I could be while serving in the United States Air Force. I served as a Fuels Specialist, and as Fuels Management Superintendent. I believe that the people whom I had the honor to serve with, trusted me and believed in me.

Ralph Riley Cooley

DEPARTMENT OF THE AIR FORCE
HEADQUARTERS STRATEGIC AIR COMMAND
OFFUTT AIR FORCE BASE, NEBRASKA, 68113

2 MAR 1978

MSgt Ralph R. Cooley
509th Supply Squadron
Pease AFB, NH 03801

Dear Sergeant Cooley

It is a pleasure to inform you that you have been selected as the SAC Outstanding Fuels Manager of the Year (Superintendent) 1977. This recognition is a result of your outstanding contributions to the SAC mission and places you in a distinctive group of dedicated personnel who have been previously selected for this award.

The criteria for determining this award insure that none but the most highly qualified are nominated. To be chosen is indeed a very great honor and an outstanding accomplishment.

I am proud to have an individual of your caliber assigned to this command. I extend my congratulations and appreciation for a job well done.

Sincerely

Martin C. Fulcher

MARTIN C. FULCHER
Major General, USAF
Deputy Chief of Staff, Logistics

Peace . . . . is our Profession

NARRATIVE

PERFORMANCE OF DUTIES: SMSgt Cooley's duty performance is consistently outstanding. He is the driving force that made the 81st Supply Squadron Fuels Management one of the leading fuels accounts in the United States Air Forces Europe. Over the last year, he has supervised the safe receipt and issue of over 20 million gallons of fuel. In the absence of a fuels officer he singlehandedly managed this diverse twinbase fuels operation for nearly 3 months. During this time -- handling the work of both an authorized Captain and a Chief Master Sergeant -- he effectively sustained the fuels operations at a high level. Only through utilizing his extensive management knowledge and demonstrating dedication and hard work could he have done this in such a superior fashion. CONTRIBUTIONS TO IMPROVING FUELS OPERATIONS: SMSgt Cooley stays actively involved in all phases of Fuels Management. He identified an operational shortfall in the fire suppression system of the Type IV Hydrant Refueling System that makes "hot" refueling unsafe in heavy westerly winds. After coordinating with the Fire Department to correct the problem, he devised interim measures using a weather notification system which alerts a fire truck to standby at the "hot pit" whenever winds reach 15 knots. This system has ensured maximum safety for aircrews conducting hot" refueling. During this last year, he completed the monumental task of finalizing the Joint Support Plans (JSP) for four Forward Operating Locations (FOL) and two Colocated Operating Bases. These complex JSPs clearly define the responsibilities, requirements, and shortfalls of the United States Air Force and the other North Atlantic Treaty Organization country. His tactful and diplomatic approach in dealing with the host nation officers established excellent rapport and ensured the accuracy of the JSPs. He then closely monitored the requisitioning of the needed War Reserve Materiel (WRM) equipment to ensure fullfillment of the JSP requirements. SMSgt Cooley also has a deep regard for people and is totally involved in insuring that airmen receive the best possible training. As a direct result seven attained an above 90 score on their 63150 CDC End of Course exams. He is a most positive force in boosting the branch's morale. Paying close attention to each airman, fully uses his experience and training to help them cope with the problems they face. He also instituted a self-help program that included significant improvements in all sections of the branch. This self-help program has been a source of pride for all fuels personnel -- earning accolades of the Wing Civil Engineer. Undoubtedly, his enthusiasm and intense efforts resulted in capture of the coveted Third Air Force Golden Drum Award for fuels operational and management excellence in 1982. PARTICIPATION IN COMMUNITY ACTIVITIES: SMSgt Cooley and his family are active members of the RAF Bentwaters Protestant Chapel, teaching Sunday School and regularly attending prayer breakfasts. He and his wife actively promote Anglo-American relations through membership in a community hourseman's club. Starting the softball season as coach of the squadron softball team, he stressed the basics for a team that went on to capture first place in their league. His outstanding coaching abilities were subsequently recognized by selection as coach of the Wing baseball team. Although maintaining a busy work schedule, he is a prime example of a person who finds time to support both his church and community. OTHER NOTEWORTHY ACHIEVEMENTS: SMSgt Cooley prides himself on his indepth management background gained through Air Force training and collegiate classes. He is currently working towards a Bachelor's Degree in Sociology from Troy State University and a degree in Fuels Distribution Technology with the Community College of the Air Force. SMSgt Cooley is a professional in every sense and is eminently qualified to represent the United States Air Force as the Fuels Superintendent of the Year for 1982.

LGS

Outstanding USAF Fuels Manager of the Year Award (Superintendent Category) 1982

HQ 3AF/LGSF

Senior Master Sergeant Ralph R. Cooley is nominated as the 81st Tactical Fighter Wing representative for the Outstanding USAF Fuels Manager of the Year Award (Superintendent Category) 1982. Sergeant Cooley's loyalty and dedication to the United States Air Force are unsurpassed. His managerial expertise insured safe and timely wing A-10 fuels support for achievement of a USAF peacetime flying record of 53,000 hours. He is fully deserving of recognition as the Outstanding USAF Fuels Superintendent of the Year 1982.

DALE C. TABOR, Colonel, USAF
Commander

3 Atch
1. Narrative
2. Biography
3. Citation

V. COMMENTS OF REPORTING OFFICIAL (Be factual and specific. Add any comments which increase the objectivity of the rating...)

FACTS AND SPECIFIC ACHIEVEMENTS: SSgt Cooley continuously performs an outstanding job as a Shift Leader. He has proven to be a creative NCO with an inquisitive mind, ~~who has~~ an ability to visualize the necessity for corrective and other action. He is always one step ahead. This is evidenced by the error free support that he has rendered to aircraft of the Presidential Fleet, Heads of State, Congressmen and visiting dignitaries to the Nation's Capitol. This is an outstanding accomplishment, for approximately 85% of this type of servicing is on a no-notice basis, in which he has maintained a request delivery time of less than ten minutes per aircraft servicing, without compromise to safety. He has proven this accomplishment during a period of Presidential Inauguration and the death of Gen Dwight D. Eisenhower, as dignitaries attended the two services, arrived and required service for their aircraft. He is quiet and mannerly, but his resourcefulness, enthusiasm and ingenuity inspire confidence in his associates. His attention to duty and common sense approach to problems have demonstrated his ability as an outstanding NCO. STRENGTHS: SSgt Cooley is a very aggressive individual, whose initiative stands out among his contemporaries. His manner, dress, bearing and behavior, both on and off duty are outstanding. He is a mature individual with outstanding growth potential. OTHER COMMENTS: Based on his demonstrated performance and growth potential, I highly recommend him for promotion to E-6.

VI. REPORTING OFFICIAL

NAME, GRADE AND ORGANIZATION	DUTY TITLE	SIGNATURE / DATE
ADAM J.T. MAURER, TSgt 1001st Supply Sq	Asst.NCOIC Distribution	Adam J.T. Maurer 14 Apr 69

VII. INITIAL INDORSING OFFICIAL

The initiative, drive, and determination displayed by this NCO have served to allow more effective accomplishment of the refueling mission. He can take pride in his part in the outstanding fuel support rendered on Andrews. I concur in recommendation for early promotion.

NAME, GRADE AND ORGANIZATION	DUTY TITLE	SIGNATURE / DATE
THEODORE W. ROSIER, MSgt 1001st Supply Sq	NCOIC Distribution	Theodore W Rosier 15 Apr 69

VIII. ADDITIONAL INDORSEMENT

SSgt Cooley's close cbservance of operator performance of aircraft servicings has resulted in continued effective, efficient and safe support of all refueling requirements. Conscientiousness and dedication to outstanding service are two of the more notable traits of the outstanding NCO. I most definitely concur in his consideration of early advancement to E-6.

NAME, GRADE AND ORGANIZATION	DUTY TITLE	SIGNATURE / DATE
RICHARD C. DISCHLER, Maj 1001st Supply Sq	Fuels Manager	15 Apr 69

IX. ADDITIONAL INDORSEMENT

NAME, GRADE AND ORGANIZATION	DUTY TITLE	SIGNATURE / DATE

REVIEWED BY OER/AFB

(THIS FORM IS SUBJECT TO THE PRIVACY ACT OF 1974 - USE BLANKET PAS - AF FORM 11.)

REQUEST AND AUTHORIZATION FOR TDY TRAVEL OF DOD PERSONNEL
(Reference: Joint Travel Regulations)
Travel Authorized as Indicated in Items 2 through 21.

1. DATE OF REQUEST: 30 Nov 81

REQUEST FOR OFFICIAL TRAVEL

2. NAME (Last, First, Middle Initial) AND SSAN: SEE REVERSE
3. POSITION TITLE AND GRADE OR RATING: SEE REVERSE
4. OFFICIAL STATION: RAF BENTWATERS, ENGLAND
5. ORGANIZATIONAL ELEMENT: SEE REVERSE
6. PHONE NO.: 2106
7. TYPE OF ORDERS: ROUTINE
8. SECURITY CLEARANCE: SEE REVERSE
9. PURPOSE OF TDY: MSN

To perform JSP Site Survery and Host Nation Support Model Study.

10. APPROX. NO. OF DAYS OF TDY (Including travel time): 5
11. PROCEED O/A (Date): 1 December 1981

ITINERARY [X] VARIATION AUTHORIZED

FROM: RAF BENTWATERS, ENGLAND
TO: OTU 10 JEVER GERMAN AIR BASE, GERMANY
RETURN TO: RAF BENTWATERS, ENGLAND

12. MODE OF TRANSPORTATION

COMMERCIAL				GOVERNMENT			PRIVATELY OWNED CONVEYANCE (Check one)
RAIL	AIR	BUS	SHIP	AIR	VEHICLE	SHIP	RATE PER MILE:

[ ] MORE ADVANTAGEOUS TO GOVERNMENT

[ ] AS DETERMINED BY APPROPRIATE TRANSPORTATION OFFICER (Overseas Travel only)

[ ] MILEAGE REIMBURSEMENT AND PER DIEM LIMITED TO CONSTRUCTIVE COST OF COMMON CARRIER TRANSPORTATION AND RELATED PER DIEM AS DETERMINED IN JTR. TRAVEL TIME LIMITED AS INDICATED IN JTR.

13. [X] PER DIEM AUTHORIZED IN ACCORDANCE WITH JTR.
[ ] OTHER RATE OF PER DIEM (Specify)

14. ESTIMATED COST

PER DIEM	TRAVEL	OTHER	TOTAL	15. ADVANCE AUTHORIZED
$ 1020.00	$ -0-	$ 522.00	$ 1542.00	$

16. REMARKS (Use this space for special requirements, leave, superior or 1st-class accommodations, excess baggage, registration fees, etc.) (Prior to travel overseas comply with the Foreign Clearance Guide for passport, immunization, and clearance requirements. Attach receipts showing cost of all lodgings used during the period of this claim. Submit Travel Voucher within 5 workdays after completion of travel.)

Item 15 on reverse applies. Major Peter A. Clement, is designated as a classified courier IAW AFR 205-1. Members will utilize host nation deductible noon meal Monday thru Friday at Leipheim and Jever and Monday thru Thursday at Ahlhorn. With concurrence of Commanders concerned.

AUTHORITY: AFR 39-11 and AFR 36-20.

17. REQUESTING OFFICIAL (Title and signature): DORRAL J. CALVERT, Lt Colonel, USAF
Asst Deputy Commander for Resource Management

18. APPROVING OFFICIAL (Title and signature): [signature]

AUTHORIZATION

19. ACCOUNTING CITATION:
DEPARTMENT OF THE AIR FORCE 5723400 302 8030 XXXXXX 02 40739 40839
HQ 81ST CMBT SPT GP 40939 S666700 (11-102)
APO NEW YORK 09755 ...C: 4 4 280 02XX 666700
TDM: FOR THE COMMANDER ... RAND, SMSGT CERT OFFICER DISTRIBUTION "A"

20. ORDER-ISSUING OFFICIAL: ROBERT J. DEMMEL, ..., USAF
Chief, Central Base Administration

OFFICIAL

21. DATE ISSUED: 30 Nov 1981

22. TRAVEL ORDER NUMBER: TA-2775

DD FORM 1610 REPLACES AF FORM 626, JUN 76, WHICH IS OBSOLETE.

TEMPORARY DUTY BACK

CONTINUATION OF REVERSE TRAVEL ORDER

NAME	SSAN	GRADE	BAS CODE	RC/CC	ORGN	SCTY CLN
CLEMENT, PETER A.		MAJOR		331210	81TFW/LGX (USAFE)	TOP SECRET
NORTON, MICHAEL J.		MAJOR		334140	81TFW/LGS (USAFE)	TOP SECRET
JENSEN, TERRY W.		CAPTAIN		334240	81TFW/LGT (USAFE)	TOP SECRET
RICHARDS, WALTER JR.		CMSGT	BAS-B	344600	81CSG/SV (USAFE)	SECRET
COOLEY, RALPH R.		SMSGT	BAS-B	334110	81TFW/LGSF (USAFE)	SECRET
O'CONNOR, EDWARD B.		SMSGT	BAS-B	322E30	81TFW/EMS (USAFE)	TOP SECRET
ROGERS, GRAHAM A.		SMSGT	BAS-B	322100	81TFW/MAAM (USAFE)	SECRET
BENSON, STEVEN R.		TSGT	BAS-B	344422	81CES/DEECX (USAFE)	SECRET
PENNISTON, JAMES W.		SSGT	BAS-B	344350	81CSG/SPPX (USAFE)	TOP SECRET

NOTE: Only those items referenced in the order are applicable.

1. The verbal order of the commander on date shown in the "EFFECTIVE ON OR ABOUT" block is confirmed, exigencies of the service having been such as to preclude the issuance of competent written orders in advance. (Do not use this statement on blanket/repeated TDY orders.)
2. Justification for determining the special authorization(s) in this order is maintained in:
3. Travel permitted by this order does not entitle traveler to expenses of travel or per diem.
4. Submit a "No-Pay" voucher within 5 workdays after completion of travel. (For permissive TDY orders & TDY orders authorizing travel at no expense to the government.)
5. Reimbursement of transportation expenses necessarily incurred in the conduct of official business in and around a temporary duty station is authorized. (Public transportation only) Common Carrier.
6. Travel in connection with meetings per AFR 30-9 not authorized by this order. (Use on blanket orders)
7. If government transportation is not available, a statement of non-availability must be obtained from TMO.
8. Berlin documentation will be obtained before travel via land route to or from Berlin, Germany.
9. Within overseas area of TDY, travel by military and commercial aircraft, commercial rail, and bus is authorized.
10. Travel by commercial rail, bus or air is authorized within the CONUS.
11. Hire of special conveyance: (a) for use within area of TDY station authorized as more advantageous to the Govt (b) authorized as more advantageous to the Gov. (c) billing for hire of GSA vehicles (Gov-Owned) will be forwarded to: (NOTE: (c) with address must be included when hire of any U-drive spec convey is authorized.)
12. Use of taxi authorized as more advantageous to the Gov for official travel in the vicinity of TDY station(s).
13. Use of POV authorized as more advantageous to the Gov for official travel in the vicinity of TDY station(s).
14. "LA PERSONA A QUIEN ESTA ORDEN PERTENEZCA ESTA AUTORIZADA POR LAS AUTORIDADES MILITARES COMPETENTES DE LOS ESTADOS UNIDOS DE AMERICA PARA ENTRAR O SALIR DE ESPAÑA EN MISION OFICIAL VESTIDO DE CIVIL O MILITAR". (Required when traveling to/from Spain.)

15. NATO TRAVEL ORDER (For US Military only)
(See designation and location of headquarters on front of order)

NATO TRAVEL ORDER
ORDRE DE MISSION OTAN
NATO MARSCHBEFEHL

Country of Origin THE UNITED STATES OF AMERICA — Order Number) See Reverse
Pays de provenance LES ETATS-UNIS Numero de serie)
Ursprungsland DIE VEREINIGTEN STAATEN VON AMERIKA — Anweisungsnr.) See Reverse

1. The bearer)
Le porteur)
(Der Inhaber) See Reverse
will travel from) — to)
[illegible] de) — à)
wird reisen von) See Reverse — nach) See Reverse
via
via
ueber See Reverse
Date of departure, on or about)
Date du depart, le [illegible] vers le)
Voraussichtlicher Tag der Abreise) See Reverse
Expected date of return)
Date probable du retour)
Voraussichtlicher Tag der Rueckkehr) See Reverse
2. Authority (is) (is not) granted to possess and carry arms.
Autorisation de port d'arme (accordée) (non accordée).
Es (ist) (ist nicht) gestattet, Waffen zu besitzen und zu tragen.

3. The person named in paragraph 1 is authorized to carry)
La personne indiquée au paragraphe 1 est autorisée à porter)
Der in paragraph 1 genannten Person ist es erlaubt,
sealed dispatches, containing only official documents, numbered)
plis scellés, ne contenant que des documents officiels, numérotés)
numerierte versiegelte Sendungen, die nur dienstliche Dokumente enthalten, mit sich zu fuehren.
4. I hereby certify that this individual is a member of a Force as defined in the NATO Status of Forces Agreement, and that this is an authorized move under the terms of the Agreement.
Je soussigné certifie (par la présente) que le porteur fait partie d'une Force Armée tombant sous la définition de l'Accord de l'OTAN sur le statut des Forces Armées, et que ce déplacement est autorisé par les termes de cet accord.
Hiermit bescheinige ich, dass die genannte Person Mitglied einer Streitkraft ist, gemaess der Definition im NATO-Truppenstatut und dass diese Reise im Einklang mit den Bestimmungen dieses Abkommens erfolgt.

FOR THE COMMANDER:
See Reverse — (OFFICER AUTHORIZING MOVEMENT) (OFFICIER AUTORISANT LE MOUVEMENT) (OFFIZIER DER DIESE REISE GENEHMIGT)
Date of issue)
Date de l'autorisation)
Ausstellungsdatum) See Reverse

USAFE FORM FEB 80 453 — PREVIOUS EDITION MAY BE USED

Air Force basic training, 1961. age 20.

About the Author

Ralph Riley Cooley is a retired US Air Force airman. He was honorable discharged on January 1, 1986. He started his own business in 1988. He was a sub contractor, helping build roads and highways, using heavy trucks and heavy equipment. This was the most enjoyable job, and it had the potential to be the most lucrative job he had ever known. Due to an injury and a work stoppage on this type of work in his area, he had to look for something else.

Ralph has a strong belief system. He believes in the holy trinity, The Father, Son and Holy Spirit. He believes in family because family knows you better than anyone else. He believes that right over wrong leads to a more profound life. He has never been incarcerated, and neither has he ever put an illegal drug in his body. He whole heartedly believes a good education for all, with diversity, can lift up the standards of a family, a city, a nation.

Ralph Riley also believes in the old gospel song, *Where He Leads Me I Will Follow*. When God asked Ralph to follow him to work in a nursing home and a mental hospital, behind the doors of misery, pain, and sadness, Ralph said he almost questioned God's authority. Yet, he obeyed. Ralph Riley believes God gave him the strength and conscious to aid and comfort the acute and chronically mentally ill through the gifts of the spirit, love, joy, peace, patience, kindness, gentleness, goodness, faithfulness and self-control. Of these, patience, kindness, gentleness and self-control were his closest allies. Many prayers for the patients, staff, and for himself were always on his schedule.

Having been blessed to be physically strong and mentally alert all of his life, it was time for Ralph Riley to give back. He did just that. He gave back fifteen of his retirement years. Now, all that's left to give, are his prayers-and these few words:

"Take care of your mental health. By all means, take care of your mental health. Its an unparalleled gift from God (see chapter 25).

Ralph Riley believes this is Gods mandate to all of us!

www.ingramcontent.com/pod-product-compliance
Lightning Source LLC
Chambersburg PA
CBHW060534130626
46553CB00002B/742